Digital Supply Chain Transformation

Emerging Technologies for Sustainable Growth

Edited by
Yingli Wang and Stephen Pettit

Cardiff | Gwasg
University | Prifysgol
Press | Caerdydd

Published by
Cardiff University Press
Cardiff University
PO Box 430
1st Floor, 30–36 Newport Road
Cardiff CF24 0DE
https://cardiffuniversitypress.org

First published 2022

Cover design by Hugh Griffiths
Front cover image by Getty Images

Print and digital versions typeset by Siliconchips Services Ltd.

ISBN (Paperback): 978-1-911653-34-9
ISBN (XML): 978-1-911653-37-0
ISBN (PDF): 978-1-911653-38-7
ISBN (EPUB): 978-1-911653-35-6
ISBN (Mobi): 978-1-911653-36-3

DOI: https://doi.org/10.18573/book8

The full text of this book has been peer-reviewed to ensure high academic standards. For full review policies, see https://www.cardiffuniversitypress.org /site/research-integrity/

Suggested citation:
Wang, Y., and Pettit, S. (eds.). 2022. *Digital Supply Chain Transformation: Emerging Technologies for Sustainable Growth*. Cardiff: Cardiff University Press. DOI: https://doi.org/10.18573/book8. Licence: CC-BY-NC-ND 4.0

To read the free, open access version of this book online, visit https://doi.org/10.18573/book8 or scan this QR code with your mobile device:

Contents

List of Tables   vii

List of Figures   vii

List of Acronyms   ix

Contributors   xi

**Chapter 1. Falling Behind or Riding the Waves? Building
Future Supply Chains with Emerging Technologies**   1
Yingli Wang and Stephen Pettit

  An Outlook on the Next-Generation Supply Chain   1

  Resilient Supply Chains   2

  Sustainable Supply Chains   3

  Customer-Centric Supply Chains   4

  Intelligent Supply Chains   5

  Connected and Secure Supply Chains   6

  Emerging Technologies and Their Impact on Supply Chains   7

  Cloud Computing   7

  Pervasive Computing and the IoT   8

  Artificial Intelligence   9

  Immersive Technologies   11

  Distributed Ledger Technology (DLT)   12

  Supply Chain Digital Transformation   14

  Structure and Chapters   15

  References   18

**Chapter 2. Blockchain Technology for International Trade:
Beyond the Single Window System**   23
Jeong Hugh Han

  Introduction   23

  Single Window Systems for Global Supply Chain Management   24

    Complexity of Global Supply Chain Relationships   24

    Emergence of Single Window Systems   26

*Benefits of Using Single Window Systems – a Korean Single
Window Case* 27
Limitation of Single Window Systems 27
Blockchain Technology 28
Blockchain for Supply Chain Management 28
Value of Blockchain for Cross-Border Trade 30
Extended Traceability 30
Automation Business Intelligence: Smart Contract
and Amplification of IT 31
Prevention Mechanism for Data Immutability 31
TradeLens 32
Conclusion 35
Acknowledgement 36
References 36

Chapter 3. Leveraging AI for Asset and Inventory Optimisation 39
Sid Shakya, Anne Liret and Gilbert Owusu

Introduction 39
Strategic Deployment of Assets – the IoT and Inventory Management 41
A Use Case at BT 42
Warehouse Deployment as an Optimisation Problem 43
AI Approach to Solving the Problem 43
Business Impact 45
A Use Case of Operational Replenishment of Inventories and Assets 46
A Typical Use Case 47
Asset Move for Automated Replenishment Supported by the IoT 48
Replenishment Optimisation Problem 50
AI Approach to Solving the Problem 52
Business Impact 52
Conclusion 58
References 59

Chapter 4. Digital Supply Chain Transformation 61
Frank Omare

Introduction 61
Digital Revolution 62
Accelerator #1: Digital Engagement 63
Accelerator #2: Robotic Process Automation (RPA) 63

Accelerator #3: Analytics-Driven Insight   64

Accelerator #4: Modern Digital Architecture   64

Accelerator #5: Digital Workforce Enablement   64

Accelerator #6: Cognitive Computing   64

Future Role of Procurement   65

  Pre-Merger   66

  Post-Merger   66

Building Responsible and Resilient Supply Chains   67

Responding to Climate Change   72

Relationship Between Business Behaviours and Brand Value   74

Conclusion   77

References   78

Chapter 5. An Introduction to Flexible, On-Demand Warehousing: E-Space

81

Andy Lahy, Katy Huckle, Jon Sleeman and Mike Wilson

Introduction   81

The Warehousing Industry Today   83

A New Approach: E-Space   86

Implications of E-Space for Supply Chains   87

Implications of the E-Space Model for Users   89

Industry Perspective: On-Demand Warehousing (JLL)   91

Limitations of the E-Space Model   93

Taking the Flexible Approach Even Further   95

  Pop-up Factories   95

  Distributed Manufacturing   95

  Local Sourcing   96

  Circular Economy   96

Conclusion   97

References   98

Chapter 6. Towards a Shared European Logistics Intelligent Information Space

99

Takis Katsoulas, Ioanna Fergadiotou and Pat O'Sullivan

Background and Business Context   99

  Towards Smart, Green and Integrated Transport and Logistics   99

  Industry Requirements   102

  The Shared European Logistics Information Space (SELIS) Project   102

Supply Chain Community Notes (SCNs)   103

    The SCN Premise   103

    Features of SELIS Supply Chain Community Nodes (SCNs)   104

The SELIS Project Methodology   106

Collaboration Logistics Models (CLMs)   108

    The SELIS Reference T&L Collaboration Framework   108

    SELIS EGLS   108

    SELIS Target Logistics Communities (LCs)   111

    Developing Collaborative Logistics Models   113

    Information Exchange Models, Semantics and Knowledge Graphs   114

SELIS Generic Applications and Results from Living Labs   115

Conclusions   116

References   118

Chapter 7. A Primer on Supply Chain Digital Transformation   **121**
Yingli Wang and Stephen Pettit

Digital Transformation   121

Supply Chain Digital Transformation   123

    Where Do You Start?   123

    Top Leadership Commitment and Support   124

    Translating the Strategy into Action   125

    Approaches to Supply Chain Digital Transformation   126

A Digital Transformation Framework for Supply Chain Leaders   127

    Data and Technology   128

    People   130

      Skills   130

      Culture and Behavioural Changes   130

Process   132

    Change Management   134

Conclusion   136

References   137

Index   141

List of Tables

2.1. Benefits of using the TradeLens platform   34

2.2. Paradigm shift of international trade through blockchain
technology   35

3.1. Example of service de-risking impact following asset move plan
deployment   55

4.1. Key elements of the Paris Agreement 2015   73

5.1. Requirements of an E-Space model   87

List of Figures

1.1. The key attributes of the next-generation supply chain   2

1.2. Supply chain digital transformation value framework   15

2.1. Combination of intermediaries in a cross-border supply chain   25

2.2. The basic model of a single window system   26

2.3. Representative structure of a blockchain   29

2.4. TradeLens connectivity with blockchain   33

3.1. Intuitu Strategic Planner tool   45

3.2. A design by Intuitu for 600 locations   45

3.3. AI-supported asset-constrained service flow   47

3.4. Problem statement   50

3.5. Example of report dashboard of recommended asset transfer
plan   53

3.6. Result of risk on products and asset replenishment
recommendation   54

3.7. Map from one depot for asset 7600-PFC3C-10GE   56

4.1. SAP success planning model   66

4.2. The consequences of supplier failure   68

4.3. Complexity in today's supply chain   69

4.4. Supply chain collaboration   72

4.5. Components of S&P 500 market value based on market capitalisation   74

4.6. The procurement cycle   76

5.1. Steps needed to set up a new warehouse   84

5.2. Centre of gravity analysis to select number and location of warehouses   85

5.3. A complex, nonsensical transport flow in a supply chain from China to Ireland   88

5.4. An E-Space-facilitated supply chain with transport from China to Ireland through central Europe   88

6.1. Obstacles to better horizontal and vertical supply chain collaboration   102

6.2. The SCN concept   103

6.3. The SELIS research methodology   107

6.4. The SELIS T&L collaboration framework – high-level view   109

6.5. Steps for LCM development   113

6.6. SELIS applications framework   115

6.7. Alignment of innovation roadmaps across different modes   117

7.1. Two pillars for digitalising supply chain   124

7.2. Three steps to translate strategy into action   125

7.3. Key enablers and execution principles for maximising returns on digital investment   128

7.4. A framework for supply chain digital transformation   128

7.5. An example of current value stream map (information and material flows)   133

7.6. Eight-step change model   135

List of Acronyms

5G	Fifth-generation communication technology
API	Application programming interface
AI	Artificial intelligence
AR	Augmented reality
AEO	Authorised economic operators
AV	Autonomous vehicles
B2B	Business to business
B2C	Business to consumer
B2G	Business to government
Covid-19	Disease caused by SARS-CoV-2
CPO	Chief procurement officer
CLM	Collaboration logistics model
CSR	Corporate social responsibility
DIO	Days in inventory outstanding
EC	E-commerce
E2E	End-to-end
EC	European Commission
EGLS	European green logistics strategies
FF	Freight forwarder
GPS	Global positioning system
GA	Genetic algorithm
GL	Greedy logic

GHG	Greenhouse gas
GNP	Gross national product
IoT	Internet of things
ICT	Information and communication technology
IT	Information technology
IaaS	Infrastructure as a service
KPI	Key performance indicator
KG	Knowledge graph
LoB	Lines of business
LCM	Logistics collaboration model
LSP	Logistics service provider
M&A	Mergers and acquisitions
MR	Mixed reality
MRA	Mutual recognition agreements
NCA	National Crime Agency
NCSC	National Cyber Security Centre
PaaS	Platform as a service
PCS	Port community systems
RFID	Radio frequency identification
RFI	Request for information
RFQ	Request for quotation
ROI	Return on investment
RPA	Robotic process automation
S&OP	Sale and operations planning
SLA	Service level agreement
SELIS	Shared European Logistics Intelligent Information Space
SME	Small and medium-sized enterprise
SaaS	Software as a service
SCN	Supply chain community node
TSP	Technology service providers
T&L	Transport and logistics
UNECE	United Nations Economic Commission for Europe
VR	Virtual reality
WMS	Warehouse management systems
WEF	World Economic Forum
XaaS	Anything-as-a-service

Contributors

About the Editors

Yingli Wang is a professor in logistics and operations management at Cardiff University, UK. She was awarded her PhD in logistics and operations management from Cardiff University in 2008. She has worked with many organizations including shippers, logistics service providers and IT service providers in the fields of e-logistics and e-supply chain. Her research on digitalisation in logistics and supply chain has attracted funding from various bodies including the Engineering and Physical Sciences Research Council (EPSRC), European Regional Development Funding (ERDF), Sweden Energy Agency, Welsh Government, Highways England and the Department for Transport (DfT). She has published in leading academic journals, and other recent publications include a report for Highways England on accelerating BIM adoption in the supply chain (2016), a foresight report for the Government Office for Science on the impact of emerging technologies on future mobility (2019), and a white paper on blockchain for supply chains for the World Economic Forum (WEF) (2019).

Stephen Pettit is a professor in the logistics and operations management section of Cardiff Business School, Cardiff University, UK. He was awarded a PhD from the University of Wales in 1993. He has been involved in a number of transport-related research projects including for the DfT (the UK economy's requirements for people with seafaring experience), and EU DGTREN (the 'Economic Value of Shipping to the UK Economy'; an 'Analysis of the Cost Structure of the main TEN Ports'; and 'Work Organisation in Ports'). His recent work has considered issues around humanitarian aid logistics and supply chain management. Stephen has contributed to many journal papers, conference papers and reports primarily on port development, port policy, and humanitarian aid logistics and supply chain management.

About the Contributors

Ioanna Fergadiotou holds Masters degrees in Information Technology and Management (National Technical University of Athens, Greece), and Educational Technology (University of Athens, Greece). She is an experienced consultant in the design and development of small, medium and large-scale information technology platforms and systems that are client facing. As the R&D Director at INLECOM she has overseen and managed many R&D and Innovation projects, with direct responsibility for KPIs that pertain to innovation, research outputs, PoCs, scientific excellence and scientific advancements. She has participated in over 30 national, European and international research and commercial projects, including in the fields of knowledge management, e-learning, ICT, transport and logistics. Previously she has worked for Vocational Training SA and the National Institute of Labour and Human Resources, as a project manager in various software firms and a research assistant at the University of Athens.

Jeong Hugh Han is an assistant professor at the Asia Pacific School of Logistics (APSL), Inha University, South Korea. He gained his MSc and PhD in business studies from Cardiff Business School, Cardiff University, UK. Prior to joining Inha University he participated in an EPSRC-funded research project, Defining and Exploring Communication Flexibility for Smart Logistics. His research areas include international logistics, global supply chain management, trade facilitation and the use of information technology capability for logistics and supply chain management. His work has been published in international journals including *International Journal of Production Economics, Supply Chain Management: An International Journal*, and *Electronic Commerce Research and Applications*.

Katy Huckle is an expert in strategic planning and digital transformation. She holds a BSc in Philosophy from the University of York, UK, and an MBA from the University of St Gallen, Switzerland. Katy has played a pivotal role in the development of strategic innovation at both DSV-Panalpina (formerly Panalpina) and the PARC Research Institute at Cardiff University, UK. Notable achievements include a multinational collaboration between Enterprise Ireland,

Dublin City University, Ireland and Panalpina; and her contributions to the PARC Research Centre, where she conducted a very well-received series of interviews on the topic of 'Women in Supply Chain'.

Takis Katsoulakos holds a PhD in Marine Engineering from the University of Newcastle upon Tyne, UK. He is the managing director of INLECOM Group, responsible for the development of the KBOS platform, EU projects and commercial contracts. From 1981 to 1996 he worked at Lloyds Register of Shipping, both as a senior principal surveyor and head of applied information engineering. He has served as chairman of the Board and Executive Committee of the European Software Institute (1994–1997); chairman of the Foundation of Enterprise Knowledge Development (1992–1994); and visiting professor, Computing Science Department, University of Manchester Institute of Science and Technology, UK (1995–1996). He is involved in the technical management of all INLECOM projects.

Andrew Lahy has worked in global supply chains for over 20 years, at multiple locations around the world and in different supply chain leadership roles, including strategy development, innovation introduction, operational excellence, and leading large-scale supply chain transformation programmes. Andrew has published several papers on supply chain innovation and was listed by the *Lean Management Journal* as one of the top 25 most influential people in Europe for his contributions. Andrew is currently a co-director at the PARC Institute of Manufacturing, Logistics and Inventory and has worked on various projects related to distributed manufacturing, additive manufacturing, inventory planning and optimisation and sustainable supply chains.

Anne Liret is research manager in operational transformation and artificial intelligence in BT's Applied Research. She has a PhD in AI and formal computation, and extensive experience in applying AI to transform telecommunications services operations. Her research at BT, for more than 20 years, has included problem modelling and solving using AI and optimisation techniques with a focus on resource scheduling problems in dynamic context, interactive scheduling and planning, derisking-oriented simulation, inventory management, and context-aware self-learning models for real-time diagnosis. Her models have been widely published and have helped in transforming operations in field engineering services, asset maintenance management and service assurance.

Frank Omare has over 20 years of senior line management and consulting experience in procurement and supply chain and is a Fellow of the Chartered Institute of Purchasing & Supply (FCIPS). He is a member of the Board of Trustees of Migrant Help, which offers advice and support to refugees, victims of slavery and human trafficking and asylum seekers. He is also on the Board of Migrant Help Trading, the social enterprise arm of the charity. Frank works at SAP Ariba which has the world's largest cloud-based network for business commerce. SAP Ariba affords him the opportunity to leverage his procurement and supply chain experience to collaborate with customers, helping them to understand the benefits of making an investment in leading-edge solutions that drive the recommendations to address complex business issues. His work also helps customers to understand the value of digital transformation and to prioritise sustainability as part of their organisation's values. Frank has spoken at various public events on sustainability on behalf of SAP.

Pat O'Sullivan is CTO and innovation director at INLECOM. His MSc and PhD degrees were IBM funded. Across his career he has led numerous commercial projects and teams across Ireland, UK, USA, China, Japan, Israel, France, Korea, Germany and India. His industry-leading innovation has evidenced new commercial products, services and spinouts/spin-ins, with over 335 successfully-granted patents in his own name from numerous R&D projects over 25 years. He won the Smith Testimonial Prize in 2005 and the Mullins Medal in 2006 at Engineers Ireland for commercially impacting R&D. Several of his patents have won awards for scientific innovation, advancement and scientific excellence. He has assisted in company acquisitions and subsequent IP development/integration leading to new market-leading products. His extracurricular activities include being an adjunct professor at the University of Limerick, Ireland and Waterford Institute of Technology, Ireland.

Gilbert Owusu has a PhD in applied AI and his research on applying AI technologies for transforming service operations has been widely published. He leads the Service and Operational Transformation Research in BT with a track record in applying AI, production management and operational modelling technologies to service operations. This has led to significant customer service improvements and OPEX reduction in BT's operations. He is also the co-editor of two books on service production management.

Sid Shakya has a PhD in Evolutionary Computation and his interest in the practical application of AI considers resource optimisation, demand modelling, forecasting, data analysis and simulations. He is a chief researcher at EBTIC (Emirates ICT research centre) at Khalifa University, UAE and a principal researcher at BT, leading workforce optimisation research, focused on organisational design and operational planning. He has extensive experience of applying AI techniques in business problems and expertise in state-of-art search heuristics and optimisation techniques, including nature-inspired computing and fuzzy systems. He is co-editor of a book in this area, and co-author of over 70 scientific papers.

Jon Sleeman is a director in the JLL Research team leading UK and EMEA Industrial and Logistics Research. He is a member of the Chartered Institute of

Logistics and Transport and has a MSc degree in Logistics and Supply Chain Management from the Cranfield School of Management, UK. JLL is a world leader in real estate services, delivering products and services that help real estate owners, occupiers and investors achieve their business ambitions.

Mike Wilson holds a BSc in Industrial Engineering and an MBA from Cardiff University, UK and is an honorary visiting professor at Cardiff Business School, Cardiff University, UK. He was the inspiration behind The PARC Institute of Manufacturing, Logistics and Inventory Research Centre which has developed several award-winning, original research programmes across a broad spectrum of supply chain and manufacturing. Mike was head of UK Operations for Design to Distribution, the manufacturing subsidiary of Fujitsu/ICL which subsequently became part of Celestica in the mid-1990s – one of the world's largest electronics manufacturing services providers – and ran the $3.5bn European business until 2003. He moved into Third Party Logistics with Exel as President of Technology, which subsequently became DHL. Following some time in Asia, working independently setting up manufacturing and supply chains, he joined Panalpina in 2011 as Global Head of Logistics and after the acquisition by DSV became Executive Vice President for Logistics Manufacturing Services and Latin America.

CHAPTER 1

Falling Behind or Riding the Waves? Building Future Supply Chains with Emerging Technologies

Yingli Wang and Stephen Pettit

An Outlook on the Next-Generation Supply Chain

Supply chains are constantly evolving and increasingly intertwined with the development of digital technologies. As observed by Gartner, a tremendous wave of automation and augmentation has sped through corporate supply chains in the last few years (Youssef, Titze & Schram 2019). With rapidly evolving customer demands and the emergence of new business models, organisations need to leverage these new business concepts and technologies to build new capabilities and future-proof their supply chains in order to remain competitive in the marketplace. So, what would a future supply chain look like? Figure 1.1 highlights the key attributes of a future supply chain – and each of these attributes is discussed in the following sections.

How to cite this book chapter:
Wang, Y., and Pettit, S. 2022. Falling Behind or Riding the Waves? Building Future Supply Chains with Emerging Technologies. In: Wang, Y., and Pettit, S. (eds.) *Digital Supply Chain Transformation: Emerging Technologies for Sustainable Growth.* Pp. 1–22. Cardiff: Cardiff University Press. DOI: https://doi.org/10.18573 /book8.a. Licence: CC-BY-NC-ND 4.0

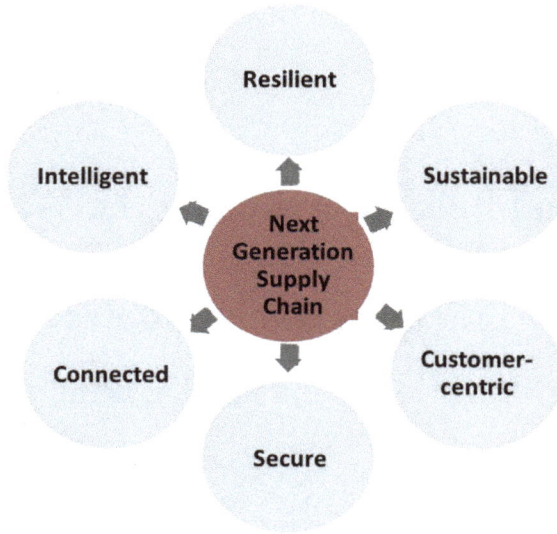

Figure 1.1: The key attributes of the next-generation supply chain. Source: Authors.

Resilient Supply Chains

Supply chains operate in a volatile world with increasing uncertainties and disruptions. These disruptions include, for instance, changing customer demand, competitors' activities, unforeseen incidents, geopolitical movements (such as the US–China trade war and Brexit), natural disasters and the current Covid-19 pandemic. Conversely, it should be noted that supply chain disruptions can also bring unexpected opportunities for success (Sheffi 2005). As has been witnessed, e-commerce fulfilment has seen significant growth during the pandemic. Nonetheless, disruptions force companies to reassess their supply chain strategies, network structures and footprints. Thus, it is of paramount importance that the next generation of supply chain be *resilient*, namely, to be able to sense, respond to and recover from disruptions by maintaining continuity of operations at the desired, or with an even better, level of connectedness and control (Ponomarov & Holcomb 2009; Tukamuhabwa et al. 2015).

A key competence or capability for supply chain resilience is agility – the ability to rapidly respond to unpredictable and constantly changing conditions. Swafford, Ghosh and Murthy (2008) argued that agility is a core competence that relies on various capabilities, specifically various forms of flexibility. They further pointed out that information technology (IT) is a key enabler to flexibility, which in turn results in higher supply chain agility. In fact, IT itself needs to be flexible in order to support effective supply chain responsiveness and performance (Han, Wang & Naim 2017). As supply chains strive to adapt to a fast-changing world, technology can play a major role in making them more agile, responsive and efficient. For example, by utilising big data analytics and machine learning, organisations could develop advanced demand sensing models that incorporate both structured and unstructured data from a variety range of sources, adding a new level of granularity and accuracy to demand forecasts. IT is also essential to building supply chain visibility. By utilising established (e.g. radio frequency identification (RFID), global positioning system (GPS) and cloud computing) and emerging technologies (e.g. digital twin and blockchain), organisations can build real-time or near-real-time visibility into their supply chain. This ability to 'see' what is happening in the supply chain across organisational boundaries improves firms' adaptability and enables them to reconfigure their supply chain resources for greater competitive advantage (Dubey et al. 2018; Wei and Wang 2010).

Sustainable Supply Chains

Nothing is more pertinent than embedding sustainability in supply chain operations. Future supply chains must incorporate not only economic but also social and environmental goals in their strategies and practices, deploying the so-called 'triple bottom line' (Elkington 1998). At the centre of the concept of the triple bottom line lies the idea that a sustainable organisation is one that creates profit for its stakeholders while protecting the environment and improving the lives of those with whom it interacts (Savitz 2013). The year 2020 marks the fifth anniversary of the adoption of the Sustainable Development Goals by the United Nations. These goals are the blueprint to achieving a better and more sustainable future for all, and therefore should be the guiding framework for all types of supply chains actors. They address the global challenges we face, including poverty, inequality, climate change, environmental degradation, peace and justice (United Nations 2020).

The growing trend of more destructive climate disasters such as the Australian bushfires and South Asian floods demonstrate all too well the urgent need for action on climate change and global warming (BBC 2020; ReliefWeb 2020). Scientists have pointed out that holding warming to 1.5°C above pre-industrial levels could limit the most dangerous and irreversible effects of climate change (IPCC 2018). This means that every part of the global economy needs to rapidly decarbonise. Climate change is already having substantial physical impacts in regions across the world, for instance severely paralysed critical transport infrastructures, which impacts on the movement of goods. Future supply chains need to adapt and adopt lower carbon strategies with conscious decisions made about their carbon footprints. This requires strategies that use more renewable resources and eliminate waste from end-to-end supply chains. They will also need to have embedded in them the principles of the circular economy, which advocates for the change from a linear 'take–make–use–dispose' consumption model to a circular one. This principle aims to keep resources in use for as long as possible, extract the maximum value from them while in use, then recover and regenerate products and materials at the end of each service life (WRAP 2020).

One notable concept, albeit one that is still in its infancy, is the idea of a 'material passport', based on the idea of the circular economy and powered by blockchain technology (Heinrich & Lang 2020). A circular supply chain underpinned by blockchain technology provides a material backbone that offers a comprehensive and trustworthy record of material composition and value throughout its life cycle. The interconnectivity and visibility at a supply chain ecosystem level will lay the foundation for the better tracking of material flows and the rates of cyclical use, reduction and disposal, and the effective set-up of a closed-loop supply chain. This will allow various sectors (for example, construction, automotive and electricals) to go beyond improving energy efficiency, transforming both asset utilisation and materials management within these sectors.

In recent years, burgeoning issues related to social sustainability have also been gaining in importance (Mani et al. 2016; Sarkis, Helms & Hervani 2010). Hutchins and Sutherland (2008) recommended several proposed measures of social sustainability for supply chain decision-making (labour equity, healthcare, safety and philanthropy) that serve as a starting point to establish a comprehensive social footprint for a company. Again, digital technology is seen as a critical enabler in areas such as using internet of things (IoT) devices for tracking and estimating possible dangers, thus increasing workplace safety.

Customer-Centric Supply Chains

Supply chain functions within organisations have shifted from inward-focused supply management to supply chains that orchestrate a profitable response to demand. Traditional customer segment and customer service management have evolved to focus on 'micro-segmentation' and 'personalisation' – tailoring products and services to individual customers' needs at *scale*. Personalisation at scale requires companies to build their agility and flexibility, supported by underlying digital capabilities. For example, with its direct-to-consumer online model, Nike allows its customers to customise their shoes based on a range of design options, achieving economies of scale and scope at the same time.

Speed in response to customer demand is also key to customer satisfaction, and it is of particular importance in business to consumer (B2C) industries. Customers want a seamless online and offline experience and demand a very short order to delivery time (for example, same-day delivery). JD.com is able to utilise its digital platform, fully automated fulfilment centre and advanced demand sensing capability to offer a same-day or next-day delivery service to

90% of its orders in China, and holds a four-minute order fulfilment record that is unlikely to be outperformed anytime soon by its e-commerce competitors (Bowden 2018).

As customers will only continue to value more personalised services and products, the demand on future supply chains to meet their expectations will only increase. To successfully ride this wave of change, companies need to continuously evaluate how digital disruption is changing customer behaviour, rethink their customer engagement model to leverage disruptive technologies, and proactively orchestrate a customer journey that goes beyond selling and maximising the value offering across the life cycle from product design to sale, use and end of life. Sharma, Gill and Kwan (2019) argued that equally important for business to business (B2B) companies is the capability to leverage the pro-liferation of enterprise internet of things (IoT), anything-as-a-service (XaaS) solutions and cloud computing to build outcome-focused customer success management – especially establishing a customer-centric digital transformation to help increase 'stickiness' and customer loyalty. They further argued that future customer touchpoints will increasingly be skewed toward digital, pro-viding a real-time customer experience that is contextualised, personalised, and driven by data and usage.

Intelligent Supply Chains

Future supply chains should be *intelligent*, in that they can sense, act and adapt autonomously without much human intervention. This may sound quite far-fetched but, after six decades of development, artificial intelligence (AI) has reached a tipping point (Wang, Skeete & Owusu 2020). As discussed later, there are a number of use cases in supply chains that could benefit greatly from AI. AI started from automating mundane and repetitive tasks back in the 1960s, and has now developed to being able to predict and prescribe intelligent recom-mendations for action, thanks to the latest developments in machine learning, increasing computing power (graphics processing unit) and the availability of big data. We will increasingly see our decisions being augmented by machine learning algorithms, human operators working alongside robots on produc-tion lines and fulfilment centres, autonomous vehicles such as truck platoon-ing, drones for delivery, and the use of chatbots for customer services.

The latest McKinsey global survey (2020) of over 2,300 participants on the state of AI identified that, in supply chains, efforts have been concentrated on two areas: logistics network optimisation, and inventory and parts optimisa-tion. For manufacturing, this has been in areas of yield, energy and/or through-put optimisation and predictive maintenance. Within these functions, the larg-est share of respondents reported revenue increases for inventory and parts optimisation, pricing and promotion, customer service analytics, and sales and demand forecasting. Over half of the respondents said that use cases on cost reduction are mostly from the optimisation of talent management, contact centre automation, and warehouse automation. Revenue increases from AI adoption in that year were more commonly reported in half of business functions, but cost decreases were less common. The survey also revealed that the adoption of deep learning (a subset of machine learning that uses artificial neural networks to analyse unstructured data inputs such as images, video and speech) was mostly at an early stage, with only 16% of respondents saying they had taken deep learning beyond the pilot stage. However, AI will be the power engine behind autonomous vehicles, robotics and a number of other use case areas in the near future. High-tech and telecom companies are 'leading the charge'. Organisations need to watch these developments closely, otherwise they may risk being left behind.

Connected and Secure Supply Chains

The foundation of resilient, sustainable, intelligent and customer-centric supply chains is supply chain connectivity and end-to-end visibility. This is best envisaged as data and information flowing through the supply chain network like water flows in a pipeline. In a fragmented supply chain, the flow tends to be interrupted frequently due to a number of barriers such as organisational silos and a lack of interoperability between IT systems. A fragmented supply chain often has a longer cycle time and is less responsive to customer needs and business disruptions. On the other hand, a highly connected supply chain allows data to flow smoothly between different functions within an organisation and between organisations. Connectivity, plus the willingness to allow information sharing, leads to much-needed supply chain visibility, which is critical for supply chain planning, execution and analytics. In an ideal state, there would be a supply chain digital twin in place, that is, a digital representation of real-world physical supply chains, including all relevant ecosystem actors (suppliers, customers, service providers and others). A digital twin allows clear visibility into complex, interconnected supply chains, and performs both optimisation of coordination for the current state and what-if analyses for the future state.

However, what supply chain executives and academia tend to forget is that a digitally connected supply chain also needs to be highly secured. Cybercrime leads to data breaches, financial crimes, market manipulation and the theft of personal data, and poses risks to public safety and security. According to a National Crime Agency report (National Crime Agency (NCA) 2017), within three months of the creation of the National Cyber Security Centre (NCSC) in June 2017, the UK was hit by 188 high-level attacks that were serious enough to warrant NCSC involvement, and countless lower-level ones, indicating that cybercrime is increasingly aggressive and frequent. The vulnerability of supply chain systems was clearly illustrated by the recent case of the NotPetya cyberattack on a number of organisations, including the world's largest container shipping line, Moller-Maersk, in June 2017. The attack affected all its business units' operations and resulted in $300 million of lost revenue (Milne 2017). The rising number of IoT devices increases security risks to supply chains because many connected devices have less secure software and are vulnerable to malware. Millions of insecure IoT devices are connected to the internet and have become the 'botnet of things', presenting 'a serious challenge to cyber security for a considerable time to come' (NCA 2017: 8). Therefore, all supply chain actors in the ecosystem should make cyber security a top priority. The UK's National Cyber Security Centre provides excellent guidance and principles on supply chain security to help organisations establish effective control and oversight of their supply chains (NCSC 2020).

Emerging Technologies and Their Impact on Supply Chains

Supply chains are experiencing the implementation of a new wave of digital technologies, ranging from AI, the IoT, digital twins, 5G, big data and advanced analytics to blockchain/distributed ledger technology. Such technological developments affect *every* industry, create disruptions, and bring profound changes to the way supply chains are configured and managed. It is widely recognised that organisations need to leverage these emerging technologies and future-proof their supply chains by transforming into digital supply chains or, in a wider sense, digital supply chain ecosystems (Garay-Rondero et al. 2020; Nasiri et al. 2020). A brief examination of some of these technological developments is now provided.

Cloud Computing

At the infrastructure level, it can be seen that the deployment of cloud computing has been adopted as for mainstream use. Using a network of remote servers hosted on the internet to store, manage and process data, cloud computing allows third parties to host ICT systems on behalf of their customers. This provides flexibility and ease of use to enable not only large companies but also small and medium-sized enterprises (SME) to adopt such systems, significantly reducing entry barriers for them and fuelling new business models pioneered by technology service providers (TSP). For example, the use of telematics and GPS for tracking tractors and trailers is well established in road freight. On-demand models promoted by TSPs allow haulage companies to lease rather than buy tracking devices, representing a significant saving on fixed assets. From infrastructure as a service (IaaS) and software as a service (SaaS) to platform as a service (PaaS), cloud computing offers a flexible technology solution for organisations, providing scalability when required. The use of cloud computing is also expected to increase with the enhanced connectivity offered by full fibre and 5G.

Cloud computing, compared with other technologies, is probably the most established technology in supply chains. The most frequently mentioned impact of cloud computing is affordability, and specifically cost savings, in terms of capital expenditure, labour costs and power and cooling costs (Leimbach et al. 2014). For SMEs, cloud computing offers a high level of security when there is a lack of in-house expertise. Cloud computing also gives organisations the flexibility to scale up or down quickly, allowing businesses to experiment and launch new services and products much more quickly. This may lead to the emergence of new start-ups and potentially new job opportunities.

Pervasive Computing and the IoT

As computing power increases, and smart devices become smaller, more affordable and capable, people and devices will become more connected than ever before. Such ubiquitous connectivity and network services enable real-time visibility across supply chains, which is critical for dealing with rising uncertainty and complexity in freight transport, especially in multimodal environments. A key enabler for such technological development is pervasive computing (Satyanarayanan 2001). The most prevalent forms of pervasive computing include ubiquitous computing,[1] ambient intelligence,[2] sentient computing[3] and the IoT. While each form has a slightly different focus, in practice all of these augment everyday objects with microelectronic sensors and actuators, and wireless communication capabilities (Bibri & Krogstie 2017). Hence, they become 'smart' objects, they 'know' where they are, which other things are in the locality (context awareness) and what happened to them in the past.

---

[1] Ubiquitous computing is a concept in software engineering and computer science where computing is made to appear everywhere and anywhere. Computers will function invisibly and unobtrusively in the background, and make everyday objects smart by enabling them to communicate with each other, interact with people and their objects, and explore their environment, thus helping people to carry out activities or tasks whenever and wherever needed.

[2] Ambient intelligence (AmI) refers to the presence of a digital environment that is sensitive, adaptive and responsive to the presence of people. This is the term preferred by the European Union.

[3] Sentient computing denotes the use of sensing devices to observe and monitor and computing devices to perceive (recognise and interpret) and react to the physical environment.

Currently, the IoT's main deployment in supply chains lies in product track-ing and monitoring, for example inventory management and control in the supply chain, real-time routing, dynamic vehicle scheduling, management of trailers, containers and other heavy assets, and shipment tracking. Railway tracks, autonomous vehicles (AVs) and flight navigation can derive further value from IoT (Manyika et al. 2015). In sectors actively exploring the use of the IoT, RFID is the most widely used smart object in supply chains. RFID tags contain embedded microchips that allow freight operators to track individual assets and containers and to determine the temperature and humidity of fro-zen or liquid goods or a vehicle's mechanical condition. One example of inno-vative IoT use is that of the German carmaker Daimler, which launched the car2go service, using IoT functionality to monitor and manage cars remotely, allowing customers to use shared cars as required. This represents a radical change in Daimler's business model, transforming it from a car manufacturer to a mobility service provider. Retailers are also at the frontier of IoT adoption. Sensors already automatically check out customers purchases and restock the retail inventory after purchase. RFID tags track inventory throughout the store, shelf sensors ensure the inventory is on display, and mobile payments reduce checkout queues.

The concept of the digital twin is closely related to the IoT. A digital twin is a virtual doppelganger of a real-world object, or a complex ecosystem of con-nected objects, such as an AV in the middle of rush-hour traffic. Engineers can analyse how a vehicle performs not just in its physical environment but over its entire life cycle. Digital twins are particularly valuable in the telecommunica-tions, transport and construction sectors, where the management of an asset's life cycle is critical to its correct functioning. The IoT, simulation software, and machine learning and predictive analytics systems are three emerging tech-nologies that enable digital twins. Although many people still interface with digital technologies via keyboards, screens etc., interfaces will not be needed in the future. Instead, we will interact with them, thanks to the instantaneous two-way communication enabled by the IoT.

Artificial Intelligence

As intelligent algorithms become more sophisticated and computing power grows significantly, machines have started to gain human-like cognition, ena-bling them to, for instance, drive trucks, aeroplanes or trains, and this led to the concept of artificial intelligence (AI). Robotics and AVs, computer vision, language, virtual agents and machine learning are the key developments of this technology (Bughin et al. 2017; Hall & Pesenti 2017). High-tech and financial services are the leading sectors for AI deployment. The automotive and assem-bly sectors were some of the first to implement advanced robotics for manu-facturing and developing self-driving cars. Retailers rely on AI-powered robots to run their warehouses, automatically ordering stock when inventories run low, and even running unmanned stores. With smartphone penetration, retailers have developed omni-channel sales strategies, which AI can help optimise, update and use to tailor sales to each shopper in real time.

Clearly, manufacturing and financial services are leading the use of AI. For manufacturers, AI is deployed to automate assembly lines, predict sales of maintenance service, and optimise route and fleet allocation for logistics activities. Transportation and logistics demonstrate a reasonable scale of AI adoption. This reflects the substantial progress made towards truck automation and platooning in recent years.[4] Truck automation requires AI to process the vast amounts of data collected by a vehicle's sensors. For example, truck automation requires spatial recognition and an understanding of the vehicle's immediate environment as well as its exact location. Limited self-driving automation requires the ability to anticipate the behaviour of other vehicles, pedestrians and animals while simultaneously considering the movement of the vehicle. Although there have been significant developments in AI, these capabilities are not fully developed (Eastwood 2017).

Another area of AI application is in robotics and warehouse automation. Articulated robots have been seen for many years in warehouses assembling pallet loads from trailers and containers. The use of next-generation robotics for online e-commerce (EC) order fulfilment is one of the new areas for further diffusion. EC orders are usually small, often requiring only one or two items to be picked up at a time. Current industrial practice of order-picking is largely manual, hence large EC fulfilment centres tend to employ hundreds of pickers and packers in order to achieve their delivery targets, particularly during peak seasons such as Christmas and Black Friday. Many have an ambitious target of 15 minutes from click to ship, which is only achievable with the use of robots (Cooper 2018). Some believe that finding labour will be more challenging following the UK's exit from the EU. This makes a more compelling case for the adoption of robotic picking. Large logistics companies such as DHL have piloted the use of autonomous robotic cobots for picking.[5] Amazon is also a pioneer in robotics, spending $775 million in 2013 to buy a start-up, Kiva, a company that builds mobile robots. These robots can pick up a shelf of goods

---

[4] 'Platooning' refers to several freight vehicles that are travelling autonomously in convoy and in communication with each other. It involves a lead truck whose human driver navigates traffic, with several trailing vehicles automatically undertaking the steering and braking required to maintain a safe (mostly fixed) distance from the vehicle in front. This concept is currently being trialled in Europe, and has the potential to increase the volume of freight traffic (SMMT 2020).

[5] 'Cobots' are collaborative robots that work side by side with human employees, supporting repetitive and physically demanding tasks in logistics.

and bring the entire shelf to the picker, who can stay in one spot to assemble the order, eliminating the need for excessive walking between aisles in a warehouse. This concept is known as 'goods-to-picker' and in some cases has led to a 50% saving in warehouse picking labour (DHL 2020).

In addition to warehouse automation, the use of AI in retailing could anticipate demand trends, optimise product assortment and pricing, personalise promotions, offer immediate assistance with virtual agents, automate in-store checkouts and complete last-mile delivery by drones. In the context of virtual assistants, the concept of 'conversational technology' emerges, powered by rich visual interfaces and AI (Mimoun & Poncin 2015). Apart from its application in education and smart homes, conversational technology has emerged in customer service (via messaging apps), allowing a continuous customer–brand conversation. These app-based, AI-driven conversations enable the brand to zoom in on what customers need, regardless of how they say it, based on an understanding of context. Such conversational technologies may diffuse into logistic areas such as warehouse picking and vehicle loading, where operators receive specific guidance and advice in real time to complete their tasks. It may be useful for simulated training and learning as well.

Although automation and AI will improve productivity and economic growth, they are not without concerns, such as the potential effects on employment. According to a recent McKinsey report, 60% of occupations have at least 30% of work activities that could be automated (Manyika et al. 2017). Even so, even with automation the demand for work and workers could increase as economies grow, partly fuelled by productivity growth enabled by technological progress. During this transition, the workforce needs to be reskilled to exploit AI, rather than compete with it, and governments with ambitious AI strategies will need to join the global competition to attract AI talent and investment. Autonomous robots powered by AI may also threaten human identity, uniqueness, safety and resources, and hence progress is required on the ethical, legal and regulatory challenges that could potentially inhibit AI. Companies also need to adapt to different ways of working, whether in integrating AI or with on-demand workers.

Immersive Technologies

Immersive technologies blur the boundary between the physical and the digital (or simulated) world to create a sense of immersion. Related terms include virtual reality (VR), augmented reality (AR) and mixed reality (MR). Such technologies provide a stimulating, multimedia digital environment for people to experience, rather than just read, watch or listen. Given that the boundaries between products, services and environments have blurred, immersive technologies are increasingly applied in practice. Currently, there is strong demand for immersive technologies from industries in the creative economy – specifically, gaming, live events, video entertainment and retail (Hall & Takahashi 2017) – but wider applications are found in the manufacturing and maintenance, tourism, healthcare, education, transport and construction industries. For example, in construction, Costain UK applied AR to its construction project at Custom House station in east London, allowing its customer Crossrail to view the planned construction works in a 3D image overlaid onto a view of the real site with an iPad (Cousins 2014).

There are subtle differences between VR, AR and MR. AR is by far the most deployed term both academically and in practice. There are limited studies on the impact of immersive technologies specifically in the logistics sector, but obvious areas of application include on-the-job training, real-time process instruction, navigation and wayfinding aids, and digital interaction with customers and partners. Cirulis and Ginters (2013) pointed out that AR could significantly improve some logistics operations, including order-picking in a warehouse using path-finding techniques. Integrated with existing technologies such as voice-picking, this could improve the productivity of the workforce and radically change the way employees perform tasks.

One example of a picking system using AR technology is KiSoft, which displays information regarding location through a head-mounted display (KNAPP 2013). The purported advantages include visual, error-free picking instructions with fully automated goods and serial-number tracking, adaptable to every warehouse without any structural changes. In the retail sector, Tesco has begun augmented technology trials, where web cameras and mobile devices view life-size projections of products before purchase. Immerseuk.org have illustrated how immersive technologies have trained ground operation crew in the aviation industry, demonstrating the value of AR for training when the real environment is potentially dangerous or noisy, or when employees are unable to experience real-life situations or learn on site. Another example is Unilever's use of collaborative robots and VR simulators to automate repetitive manual tasks and improve the safety, operation and maintenance of equipment. Its technicians use AR glasses to record and share best practice in maintenance procedures across the network (Aronow, Ennis & Romano 2017).

Distributed Ledger Technology (DLT)

Widely considered one of the most disruptive technologies, DLT (also known as blockchain technology) enables the creation of decentralised currencies such as Bitcoin, self-executing digital contracts ('smart contracts') and intelligent assets that can be controlled over the internet (Wang, Han & Beynon-Davies 2019). DLT can be perceived as another application layer that runs on top of internet protocols that enable economic transactions between relevant parties. It can also be used as a registry and inventory system for recording, tracing, monitoring and transacting assets (whether tangible, intangible or digital). From a business perspective, a blockchain is a platform whereby values are exchanged among peers without requiring any trusted third party.

There are two main types of distributed ledgers, based on access control mechanisms, regarding who can read a ledger, submit transactions to it and participate in the consensus process:

1. Public ledger: every transaction is public (permissionless) and users can remain anonymous. The network typically has an incentivising mechanism to encourage more participants to join the network. Bitcoin and Ethereum are examples.
2. Permissioned ledger: participants need to obtain an invitation or permission to join. Access is controlled by a consortium of members or by a single organisation. These are a viable option for the freight ecosystem.

Earlier versions of blockchain are permissionless: transactions are broadcast to every single participant (node) and every node thus keeps a complete record of the entire transaction history. Economic incentives are built in to encourage honest behaviour, e.g. rewarding miners with tokens. Bitcoin is a typical example of a permissionless blockchain. Later, organisations realised that, owing to the sensitive nature of their data and regulatory concerns, sometimes a public blockchain was not a feasible option. As a result, permissioned (also known as private) blockchains (where only authorised participants can join) emerged to adapt to the needs of those organisations. Most blockchain technology networks observed so far in logistics and supply chains have been permission-based – where transactions and transaction-related data are only broadcast to selected parties (those involved in a specific trade to which these transactions relate).

Typical use cases of blockchain in supply chains include:

1. Product provenance and traceability: a blockchain system offers extended visibility among multiple supply chain actors of a (digitised) product's digital footprint, from manufacturing to distribution and sale, thus creating the so-called 'see-through' supply chains. The immutability afforded by a blockchain system enhances data integrity and leads to increased confidence from customers of products' legitimacy. Moreover, the use of timestamping (the process of providing a temporal order among sets of events) in the blockchain can prove the existence of certain data at a point of time, avoiding potential conflicts and disputes between parties over time-sensitive issues. Information completeness can be enhanced as well, as blockchain can accommodate a wide range of data, including ownership, location, product specification and cost.
2. Process and operation improvement: a blockchain platform can help to ease the current heavy workload on information transfer and processing, and bring multiple stakeholders together by the digitalisation of docu-

ment transfers and the acceleration of the flow of data. A typical example often cited in the literature is IBM's cross-border platform enabled by blockchain.

3. Automation and smart contracts. Current operations, processes and data exchanges in logistics and supply chains are often manual, slow and error-prone. With smart contracts, blockchain technology allows for increased automation and efficiency through avoiding the rekeying of data, speeding up of transactions and reduction of errors. In the blockchain context, smart contract is a computer code running on top of a blockchain containing a set of rules under which the parties to that smart contract agree to interact with each other. If and when the predefined rules are met, the agreement is automatically enforced. The smart contract code facilitates, verifies and enforces the negotiation or performance of an agreement or transaction.

4. Trade finance and settlement: blockchain used in trade finance mainly focuses on removing inefficiencies from existing processes. For example, blockchain can be used for faster credit risk assessment, minimising human errors in documentation checks, instant verification and reconciliation of records, automatic execution of workflow steps via smart contracts, and instant and secure exchange of data.

5. Anticorruption and humanitarian logistics: in a blockchain, unethical or opportunistic behaviours are made visible to all participants. This level of transparency can be of great value to traditional supply chains, such as in pharmaceuticals, where dominant supply chain actors may manipulate the market to inflate product prices, or in coffee supply chains, where a fairer payment to farmers can be made visible to relevant stakeholders. Similarly, a blockchain system could help to expose and eliminate corruptions that are witnessed in certain public–private interactions. In a similar vein, blockchain has been deployed in humanitarian supply chains to ensure that financial or other emergency aid reaches the target beneficiaries.

Supply Chain Digital Transformation

Supply chains are inherently complex and difficult to transform. Achieving a completely smooth operation and building the next-generation supply chain with the aforementioned attributes is incredibly hard but not impossible. Figure 1.2 attempts to offer a structured way for supply chain digital transformation based on the concept of business model (Wang, Chen & Zghari-Sales 2020). A starting point should be to re-examine the business value proposition – again, to have a customer-centric mindset. No matter which value proposition an organisation uses to become a digital supply chain, it will create an impact and cause changes in strategy and other parts of the business and operating models. For supply chain practitioners, this often starts by asking what

Value Network & Value
Delivery Architecture

Value Proposition	**2** What activities could help satisfy those needs?	Value Appropriation
1 What customer needs will the business model address?	**3** How could the activities be linked?	**5** How will value be created for each stakeholder?
	4 Who should perform the activities?	**6** What revenue and cost sharing models can be adopted to complement the business model?

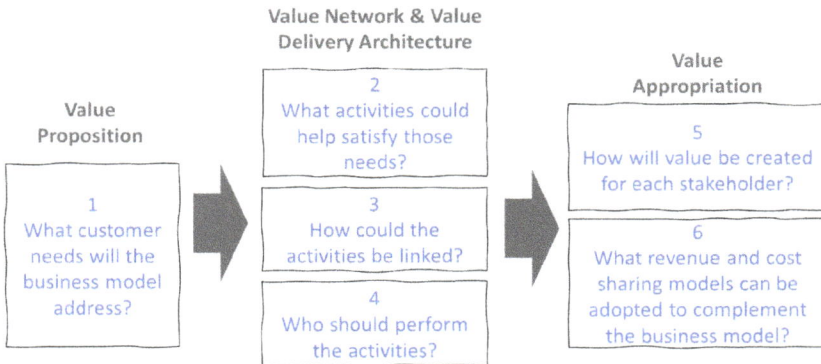

Figure 1.2: Supply chain digital transformation value framework. Source: Authors.

the pain points in the current supply chain are or whether there is an unmet (or poorly met) demand.

Once a value proposition is developed, one should move to examine how supply chains should be configured in a way that multiple supply chain actors are interconnected to coordinate and collaborate to deliver the proposed value. This is to do with process and information flow orchestration. Value network and delivery architecture are concerned with a bundle of specific activities conducted to satisfy the perceived needs of the market, along with the specification of which parties (a company or its partners) conduct which activities, and how these activities are linked to each other. Lastly, there is a need to craft a revenue mechanism and to appropriately decide and agree upon cost and benefit sharing. This is extremely important as most supply chain digital initiatives will have to involve different supply chain actors. If the investment is heavily skewed towards a particular group of supply chain actors and benefits are not distributed fairly, there is a great danger that the consortium network would collapse.

Structure and Chapters

In the context of the many challenges outlined above, the consistent and common theme running throughout is the rapid rate of change occurring. There is no doubt that existing ways of working, which have already been impacted in many ways, will continue to change rapidly over the next decade. The rate of change now, compared to even at the turn of the 21st century, means that many activities are conducted in substantially different, and in some cases almost unrecognisable, ways. Such changes will allow many companies to thrive and increase in size: witness, for example, the growth of companies such as

Amazon, which, from starting in 1994 selling books, is now a global company dominating online sales in multiple retail areas. Similarly, although at a smaller scale, grocery retailers such as Ocado have entered the market and utilised technology to disrupt the existing model of sales. Amazon and Ocado, among many other digitally driven companies, are beginning to render the long-established high street sales model redundant. Such companies are impacting how supply chains operate and, throughout the chapters that follow, we present examples of key areas where digital innovation is a necessary consideration for effective logistics practices, and where systems may already be embedded in supply chain activities.

In Chapter 2, Jeong Hugh Han considers how supply chains can be made more efficient in order to achieve the objective of maximising the stakeholders' economic profitability, while meeting the diverse range of customer requirements. The underlying discussion pertains to the role of emergent blockchain technology, which is beginning to influence how firms and IT service suppliers improve supply chain agility and flexibility using blockchain. He goes on to discuss the role of blockchain in global supply chain management and cross-border trade and explores the future of supply chains underpinned by blockchain.

Chapter 3 considers how AI can be used to optimise assets and inventory. Sid Shakya, Anne Liret and Gilbert Owusu look at how a business such as BT deals with the key resources that service organisations such as telecommunications companies maintain, that is, their assets and inventories. In the discussion they address both strategic and operational dimensions of the deployment challenge for such companies. From a strategic perspective, there is a need to deploy fixed assets for optimal performance, while at the same time from an operational perspective there is a need to replenish inventory to be able to deliver services in line with customer service level agreements. This creates a 'combinatorial optimisation problem', which it is suggested makes AI a useful technology for solving such problems for operational use.

Frank Omare demystifies digitalisation and illustrates the benefits it can bring to supply chains. In Chapter 4 he provides insights into the focus and outcomes of digitalisation and how digital failure might be avoided. As supply chains have become more complex, increased risk has been created, along with a constant pressure to monitor every aspect of the extended supply chain ecosystem. Digitalisation plays a key role in addressing visibility and transparency issues across the supply chain and helps to improve collaboration between supply chain partners to create more effective supply chains. While, for many organisations, digital transformation is a strategic imperative – improving connectivity and increasing access to, and distribution of, critical data – many organisations fail to re-engineer their business processes and dedicate insufficient resources to deploy such technology effectively.

In Chapter 5, Andy Lahy, Katy Huckle, Jon Sleeman and Mike Wilson discuss the reasons why the current 'contract logistics model' is not suitable for today's fast-moving, adaptive supply chains. The context for the chapter is how the contract logistics industry currently works, before a new model, referred to as E-Space, is introduced. The model is an attempt to redraw the existing 'contract logistics model' and implement flexible, fast and agile supply chains that can free up manufacturers and retailers to meet the short lead times consumers demand. In doing so, the model is designed to re-engineer the supply chain rather than the current contract logistics approach, which generally, in simple terms, is not adaptable. Thus, in order to meet consumer demand, supply chains have not completely changed but rather more inventory has been added in more warehouses, resulting in an 'explosion of inventory across supply chains', with products sitting in warehouses, costing money and losing value.

In Chapter 6, Takis Katsoulas, Ioanna Fergadiotou and Pat O'Sullivan look at how the European Union is developing an approach to address the substantial change taking place in the transport and logistics sector, influenced by factors such as globalisation, smart specialisation, population growth, business competition, and consumer interest for globally sourced products. The European Commission's strategy for Smart, Green and Integrated Transport and Logistics identified the need for a common communication and navigation platform for pan-European logistics. In parallel, a central goal of the Commission was to boost competitiveness in the European transport and logistics sector and develop a resource-efficient and environmentally friendly European transport system. Central to the EC's strategic vision was the development of architectures and open systems for information sharing and valorisation to connect key stakeholders on the basis of trusted business agreements. The evolving landscape set the scene for creating innovative collaboration-driven supply chain optimisation and underpinned the innovation imperatives for the Shared European Logistics Intelligent Information Space (SELIS) project, which sought to address these issues and which is discussed in this chapter.

In the final chapter, 7, Yingli Wang and Stephen Pettit reflect on what digital transformation for the supply chain has meant, and what developments in the near future might mean. While such change is primarily focused at the organisational level, it can also be stimulated at industrial or societal levels, and in order to remain competitive an organisation will have to be responsive to such pressures. The improvements in performance and competitive behaviour generated by responding to digital advances and adopting new technologies allows organisations to both raise standards and lower costs. A range of other benefits including lower market entry barriers, the creation of new value propositions, and more effective targeting of the customer base have created a more competitive landscape, and a reduction in the advantages previously enjoyed by industry incumbents. However digital transformation is a complex process. While organisations adopting new technologies might be better equipped to sustain changes in the long term, lasting performance improvements critical for success require support through a range of management approaches.

In conclusion, the latest digital developments discussed can assist the supply chain community in gaining a more precise understanding of how a business can utilise those emerging technologies to build the supply chain of the future for competitive advantage. The chapters that follow outline recent technological and theoretical issues, and present the cutting-edge and latest thinking about how those digital technologies are disrupting the existing supply chain practices in a number of areas. Awareness of the critical role of digital technologies in supporting business operations as well as driving innovations in supply chains is important for both practitioners and academics. The chapters highlight the rapid changing digital landscape in supply chains and will give readers a better understanding of what needs to be done to embrace those digital innovations to future-proof supply chains.

References

Aronow, S., Ennis, K. & Romano, J. (2017). *The Gartner Supply Chain Top 25 for 2017*. Retrieved from: https://www.gartner.com/doc/3728317?ref=SiteS earch&sthkw=internet%20of%20things&fnl=search&srcId=1-3478922254 [accessed 21 May 2018].

BBC. (2020). Australia fires: A visual guide to the bushfire crisis. Retrieved from: https://www.bbc.co.uk/news/world-australia-50951043 [accessed 11 December 2020].

Bibri, S. E. & Krogstie, J. (2017). ICT of the new wave of computing for sustainable urban forms: Their big data and context-aware augmented typologies and design concepts. *Sustainable Cities and Society, 32,* 449–474.

Bowden, G. (2018). JD.com: Inside retail's global giants. Retrieved from: https://www.retail-week.com/international/jdcom-inside-retails-global -giants/7029776.article?authent=1 [accessed 28 November 2019].

Bughin, J., Hazan, E., Ramaswamy, S., Chui, M., Allas, T., Dahlström, P., Henke, N. & Trench, M. (2017b). *Artificial intelligence: The next digital frontier*. Brussels: McKinsey Global Institute. Retrieved from: https://www .mckinsey.com/~/media/McKinsey/Industries/Advanced%20Electronics /Our%20Insights/How%20artificial%20intelligence%20can%20deliver %20real%20value%20to%20companies/MGI-Artificial-Intelligence -Discussion-paper.ashx [accessed 21 May 2018].

Cirulis, A. & Ginters, E. (2013). Augmented reality in logistics. *Procedia Computer Science, 26* (Supplement C), 14–20. DOI: https://doi.org/10.1016/j .procs.2013.12.003 [accessed 21 May 2018].

Cooper, S. (2018, February). Robotics and the click-to-ship revolution, *Logistics Focus,* 22–23.

Cousins, S. (2014). Crossrail trials augmented reality. Chartered Institute of Building. Retrieved from: http://www.bimplus.co.uk/projects/crossrail -trials-augmented-reality-and-ibeacon-pos [accessed 21 May 2018].

DHL. (2020). The logistics trend radar, 5th edition. Retrieved from: https://www.dhl.com/global-en/home/insights-and-innovation/insights/logistics-trend-radar.html [accessed 1 December 2020].

Dubey, R., Altay, N., Gunasekaran, A., Blome, C., Papadopoulos, T. & Childe, S. J. (2018). Supply chain agility, adaptability and alignment: Empirical evidence from the Indian auto components industry. *International Journal of Operations & Production Management, 38*(1), 129–148.

Eastwood, G. (2017). The future of autonomous trucks. Automotive IQ. Retrieved from: https://autonomous-commercial-vehicles.iqpc.de/report-on-the-future-of-autonomous-trucks?-ty-m&additional=true [accessed 20 December 2017].

Elkington, J. (1998). Partnerships from cannibals with forks: The triple bottom line of 21st-century business. *Environmental Quality Management, 8*(1), 37–51.

Garay-Rondero, C. L., Martinez-Flores, J. L., Smith, N. R., Morales, S. O. C. & Aldrette-Malacara, A. (2020). Digital supply chain model in Industry 4.0. *Journal of Manufacturing Technology Management, 31*(5), 887–933.

Hall, S. & Takahashi, R. (2017). Augmented and virtual reality: The promise and peril of immersive technologies. Retrieved from: https://www.mckinsey.com/~/media/McKinsey/Industries/Technology%20Media%20and%20Telecommunications/Media%20and%20Entertainment/Our%20Insights/Augmented%20and%20virtual%20reality%20The%20promise%20and%20peril%20of%20immersive%20technologies/Augmented-and-virtual-reality.pdf [accessed 11 December 2020].

Hall, W. & Pesenti, J. (2017). *Growing the artificial intelligence industry in the UK*. London: HM Government. Retrieved from: https://www.gov.uk/government/publications/growing-the-artificial-intelligence-industry-in-the-uk [accessed 21 May 2018].

Han, J. H., Wang, Y. & Naim, M. (2017). Reconceptualization of information technology flexibility for supply chain management: An empirical study. *International Journal of Production Economics, 187*, 196–215.

Heinrich, M. & Lang, W. (2020). Material passports – best practices. Retrieved from: https://www.bamb2020.eu/topics/materials-passports [accessed 15 November 2020].

Hutchins, M. J. & Sutherland, J. W. (2008). An exploration of measures of social sustainability and their application to supply chain decisions. *Journal of Cleaner Production, 16*(15), 1688–1698.

IPCC (Intergovernmental Panel on Climate Change). (2018). IPCC special report, Global warming of 1.5 °C. Retrieved from: https://www.ipcc.ch/sr15 [accessed 8 December 2020].

KNAPP. (2013). KiSoft Vision: Augmented reality. Retrieved from: http://www.knapp.com/glossary?iD=35 [accessed 15 March 2013].

Leimbach, T., Hallinan, D., Bachlechner, D., Weber, A., Jaglo, M., Hennen, L., Nielsen, R. O., Nentwich, M. Strauss, S., Lynn, T. & Hunt, G. (2014). *Potential and impacts of cloud computing services and social network websites*. European Parliamentary Research Service (EPRS) report PE 513.546.

Retrieved from: www.europarl.europa.eu/RegData/etudes/.../IPOL-JOIN
_ET(2014)513546_EN.pdf [accessed 8 January 2018].

McKinsey. (2020). Global survey: The state of AI in 2020. Retrieved from: https://
www.mckinsey.com/business-functions/mckinsey-analytics/our-insights
/global-survey-the-state-of-ai-in-2020 [accessed 8 December 2020].

Mani, V., Gunasekaran, A., Papadopoulos, T., Hazen, B. & Dubey, R. (2016).
Supply chain social sustainability for developing nations: Evidence from
India. *Resources, Conservation and Recycling, 111*, 42–52.

Manyika, J., Chui, M., Bisson, P., Woetzel, J., Dobbs, R., Bughin, J. & Aharon, D.
(2015). *IoT: Mapping the value beyond the hype*. McKinsey Global Institute.
Retrieved from: https://www.mckinsey.com/business-functions/digital
-mckinsey/our-insights/the-internet-of-things-the-value-of-digitizing-the
-physical-world [accessed 22 May 2018].

Manyika, J., Lund, S. Chui, M., Bughin, J., Woetzel, J., Batra, P., Ko, R. &
Sanghvi, S. (2017). Jobs lost, jobs gained: What the future of work will mean
for jobs, skills, and wages. McKinsey Global Institute. Retrieved from:
https://www.mckinsey.com/global-themes/future-of-organizations-and
-work/what-the-future-of-work-will-mean-for-jobs-skills-and-wages
#automation [accessed 22 May 2018].

Milne, R. (2017, 6 August). Moller–Maersk puts cost of cyber attack at up
to $300m. *Financial Times*. Retrieved from: https://www.ft.com/content
/a44ede7c-825f-11e7-a4ce-15b2513cb3ff [accessed 7 October 2017].

Mimoun, M. S. B. & Poncin, I. (2015). A valued agent: How ECAs affect website
customers' satisfaction and behaviors. *Journal of Retailing and Consumer
Services, 26*, 70–82.

Nasiri, M., Ukko, J., Saunila, M. & Rantala, T. (2020). Managing the digital supply chain: The role of smart technologies. *Technovation, 96–97*, 102–121.

National Crime Agency. (2017). The cyber threat to UK business: 2016/2017
report. National Crime Agency and National Cyber Security Centre.
Retrieved from: http://www.nationalcrimeagency.gov.uk/publications/785
-the-cyber-threat-to-uk-business/file [accessed 22 May 2018].

NCSC. (2020). National Cyber Security Centre – Supply chain security guidance.
Retrieved from: https://www.ncsc.gov.uk/collection/supply-chain-security
[accessed 11 December 2020].

Ponomarov, S.Y. & Holcomb, M.C. (2009). Understanding the concept of supply chain resilience. *International Journal of Logistics Management, 20*(1),
124–143.

ReliefWeb. (2020). South Asia floods: 9.6 million people swamped as humanitarian crisis deepens. Retrieved from: https://reliefweb.int/report/bangladesh
/south-asia-floods-96-million-people-swamped-humanitarian-crisis-deepens
[accessed 11 December 2020].

Sarkis, J., Helms, M. M. & Hervani, A. A. (2010). Reverse logistics and social
sustainability. *Corporate Social Responsibility and Environmental Management, 17*(6), 337–354.

Satyanarayanan, M. (2001). Pervasive computing: Vision and challenges. *IEEE Personal Communications, 8,* 10–17.

Savitz, A. (2013). *The triple bottom line: How today's best-run companies are achieving economic, social and environmental success—and how you can too.* John Wiley & Sons, Hobken, NJ, US.

Sharma, D., Gill, J. & Kwan, A. (2019). Customer-centric digital transformation: Making customer success integral to the new organization. Retrieved from: https://www2.deloitte.com/us/en/insights/focus/industry-4-0/customer-centric-digital-transformation.html [accessed 1 June 2020].

Sheffi, Y. (2005). *The resilient enterprise: Overcoming vulnerability for competitive advantage.* Cambridge, MA: MIT Press.

SMMT. (2020). Truck platooning: The future of road transport. The Society of Motor Manufacturers and Traders. Retrieved from: https://www.smmt.co.uk/2020/06/has-truck-platooning-hit-the-end-of-the-road/ [accessed February 2022]

Swafford, P. M., Ghosh, S. & Murthy, N. (2008). Achieving supply chain agility through IT integration and flexibility. *International Journal of Production Economics, 116*(2), 288–297.

Tukamuhabwa, B. R., Stevenson, M., Busby, J. & Zorzini, M. (2015). Supply chain resilience: definition, review and theoretical foundations for further study. *International Journal of Production Research, 53*(18), 5592–5623.

United Nations. (2020). Sustainable Development Goals. Retrieved from: https://www.un.org/sustainabledevelopment/sustainable-development-goals [accessed 11 December 2020].

Wang, Y., Chen, C. H. & Zghari-Sales, A. (2020). Designing a blockchain enabled supply chain. *International Journal of Production Research.* DOI: https://doi.org/10.1080/00207543.2020.1824086.

Wang, Y., Han, J. H. & Beynon-Davies, P. (2019). Understanding blockchain technology for future supply chains: A systematic literature review and research agenda. *Supply Chain Management: An International Journal, 24*(1), 62–84. DOI: https://doi.org/10.1108/SCM-03-2018-0148.

Wang, Y., Skeete, J. & Owusu, G. (2020). Understanding the implications of artificial intelligence on field service operations: A case study of BT. *Production Planning and Control,* in press

Wei, H. L. & Wang, E. T. (2010). The strategic value of supply chain visibility: Increasing the ability to reconfigure. *European Journal of Information Systems, 19*(2), 238–249.

WRAP. (2020). What is a circular economy? Retrieved from: https://www.wrap.org.uk/about-us/about/wrap-and-circular-economy [accessed 8 December 2020].

Youssef, M., Titze, C. & Schram, P. (2019). 2019 Gartner supply chain top 25: Europe top 15. Retrieved from: https://www.gartner.com/document/3939977?ref=TypeAheadSearch [accessed 10 December 2020].

CHAPTER 2

Blockchain Technology for International Trade: Beyond the Single Window System

Jeong Hugh Han

Introduction

There is little doubt that digitisation has been making supply chains more efficient, agile, flexible, responsive and customer-oriented. However, supply chain management is still an incomplete strategy that has not materialised its ultimate goal: to maximise overall stakeholder economic profitability while meeting diverse customers' requirements. This is mainly due to conflicts of interest among supply chain actors, lack of trust and end-to-end visibility, failure to meet ethical standards in service and production and the increasing complexity of global transactions. A growing body of literature identifies the role of blockchain technology in supporting supply chain management. In fact, there are numerous cases of firms and IT service suppliers that are already changing the way they execute agility and flexibility in their supply chains via blockchain. In this chapter, I would like to present the contents, scope and findings on the role of blockchain for global supply chain management and cross-border trade by exploring the future of the supply chain developed by blockchain, in which the autonomous linkages in the chain become the focal point of management and, thus, the transactions conducted by IT (i.e. blockchain technology) are the main concern of successful digitisation.

How to cite this book chapter:
Han, J. H. 2022. Blockchain Technology for International Trade: Beyond the Single Window System. In: Wang, Y., and Pettit, S. (eds.) *Digital Supply Chain Transformation: Emerging Technologies for Sustainable Growth*. Pp. 23–37. Cardiff: Cardiff University Press. DOI: https://doi.org/10.18573/book8.b. Licence: CC-BY-NC-ND 4.0

Single Window Systems for Global Supply Chain Management

Global supply chains that rely on extremely complex transactions between trading partners should be supported by IT in order to achieve efficient information sharing between said partners, private intermediaries and government bodies. The single window system has emerged as an IT solution for global trade that allows trading partners to share and exchange trade-related information while also conducting electronic transactions with each other.

Complexity of Global Supply Chain Relationships

The supply chain is the network of organisations that are involved in the different processes and activities that produce value and services in the hands of the ultimate customers. It includes the sequence of events in a goods flow that adds to the value of a specific good. At a national level, a domestic supply chain has the advantages of the structure of the national market, infrastructure and elements, such as the supply chain requirement under the national government, a common language, taxation levels and so on. Moreover, the short lead times and good communication in a domestic supply chain enable it to react quickly to disruption. However, in today's global setting, where the supply chain becomes international, the interactions become more dynamic, difficult to coordinate and complex than in a domestic supply chain. For example, through the different taxes, duties, transport prices, government stability and general infrastructure of a particular country, each distant market's trade law, transport regulations, product regulations, agency law, quotas, language barriers and currency issues add to the complexity of international trade (Branch 2009).

Classifying stakeholders into private and public types is illustrative of this complexity. First, the *private sector* category must include traders, such as exporters and importers, as well as intermediaries, such as the freight forwarders (FF), carriers and financial institutions involved in the commercial transactions. The primary objective for both exporters and importers is to manage the movement of products for the least possible cost and in the least possible time. Freight forwarders work directly on behalf of importers, while commercial payments and insurance contracts are managed by financial institutions. Second, the *public sector* category consists of customs and inspection agencies and port authorities. These institutions oversee legal requirements, such as inspections, tax payments and security issues, all of which create delays and add costs affecting the chain's efficiency and performance. The range of organisations involved in cross-border supply chains are shown in Figure 2.1 (Grainger 2007).

Given the above, on a global scale, supply chains require cooperation among trading partners, intermediaries and government bodies, as *international*

Shipment

Global Freight Forwarding Company/ Transport Integrator

Seller (Country A)

Buyer (Country B)

Packing Company	Local Freight Forward	Shipping Lines	Port Stevedore	Local Freight Forwarders

Local Haulage company	Inland Port of Warehouse	Local Freight Forward	Airline	Local Haulage company	Rail Road/ Train Operator	Buyer's Own Truck

Local Haulage company	Customs brokers	Shipping agent	Shipping Line	Local Freight Forward	Warehouse

Seller's Own Truck	Global Freight Forwarding Company/ Transport Integrator	Free Zone or Customs Warehouse	Shipping Line	Bank

Local Haulage company	Local Freight Forward	Consolidator	Customs brokers	Port Operator	Shipping Line	Third Party Logistics Service Provider

Local Haulage company	Bank	Customs brokers	Airline operators	Local Freight Forward	Bank	Customs brokers

Figure 2.1: Combination of intermediaries in a cross-border supply chain. Source: Adapted from Grainger (2007).

trade comprises the entire process, from the establishment of commercial contracts to transportation to monetary flow and the imposition of cross-border regulations. Consequently, cross-border logistics is one key area of any global supply chain that should be supported by efficient IT, thereby automating and streamlining complex, interrelated cross-border transactions. For example, private intermediaries, exporters and importers must submit a great deal of information and documentation to governmental bodies to comply with regulatory requirements. On the other hand, the public sector also has its own responsibility to enhance the efficiency of the trade process for the sake of facilitating trade.

Long customs clearance times caused by insufficient communication and information sharing can lead to companies suffering from increased inventory levels, delivery delays and poor customer service. Repeated trade document submission and inefficient communication between private and public parties, as well as between private participants, can result in significant financial and operational losses within the overall chain. Owing to the complexity of most transactions, supply chain stakeholders are struggling to gain transparency and visibility in their supply chains. A recent study conducted by Microsoft (2017) revealed that, out of 408 organisations and corporations from 64 countries, 69% lacked full visibility into their supply chain, 65% experienced at least one supply chain disruption, and 41% still relied heavily on Excel spreadsheets for tracking supply chain disruptions.

Emergence of Single Window Systems

To reduce the complexity of cross-border transactions while achieving greater efficiency in supply chain management, there has been a major shift towards developing and implementing single window systems. Such systems integrate and streamline cross-border transactions by enabling information sharing. The United Nations Economic Commission for Europe (UNECE) defines a single window system as a facility that allows parties involved in trade and transport to lodge standardised information and documents with a single entry point to fulfil all import, export and transit-related regulatory requirements (UNECE 2019). The core concept of any single window system can be summarised as follows: it is any electronic system that allows traders to submit standardised forms and documents simply, thus eliminating redundant and repetitive processes and allowing them to meet regulatory requirements while improving efficiency through greater cooperation between partners. With the support of web-compatible technology and internationally accepted standards, participants can conduct transactions with each other accurately and efficiently. Consequently, administrative work, such as tracking and tracing products and financial payments, can be aligned and streamlined. Single window systems so enhance the availability of information and can simplify and expedite document exchanges between private and public sector actors or even between private intermediaries. As Figure 2.2 illustrates, this system links international supply chain participants, allowing them to connect and exchange transaction-related information.

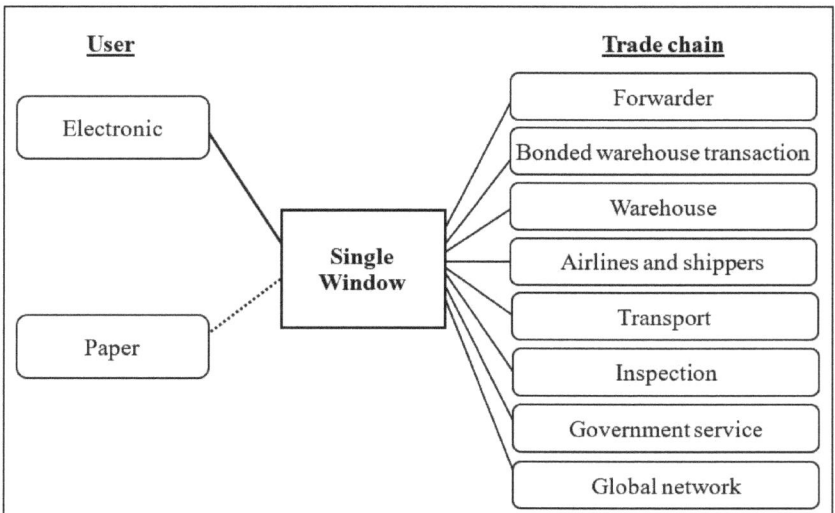

Figure 2.2: The basic model of a single window system. Source: Adapted from APEC (2007).

Benefits of Using Single Window Systems – A Korean Single Window Case

One of the representative examples of the single window system is South Korea's uTradeHub, which was launched in 2008. As Korea's ubiquitous trade hub and a single online window, it effectively connects existing trade services and simplifies international trade and logistics processes. The electronic business process of uTradeHub covers overall trade transactions, including customs clearance, logistics, banking and negotiations. The types of documents cover not only business to business (B2B) but also business to government (B2G) and government to government (G2G) trade, and uTradeHub also streamlines and speeds up the trade process with the advancement in circulation of electronic trade and logistics documents. In addition, uTradeHub acts as an official depository of electronic paperwork. A copy of all relevant paperwork for transactions is kept electronically on an isolated server. Through its services and single log-in procedure, all documents and processes for trade and logistics, such as inspection, finance and insurance, as well as other aspects of customs procedures, are all tied together and available to any supply chain participant who requires the documents. Moreover, logistics and cross-border supply chain-related information are available online in real time, so the traders and other interested parties can know exactly where they are in the customs process and keep track of cargo.

The benefits of using single window systems are diverse. The uTradeHub system makes document-handling processes more transparent and provides more links among trade participants. Moreover, as a service network, it automatically generates and processes tasks relevant to exports, imports and local affairs pertaining to trade procedures in real time, thus enabling close cooperation. Finally, the system is intuitive, as users can access it through various methods – including web portals – and exchange their information in the form of standardised documents. These benefits are directly reflected in the actual costs of trade. For example, with electronic certificates of origin, the issuance fee is cut by 50%; thus, transactions pertaining to electronic certificates of origin have increased by 200–300% each year since 2001 (UNECE 2011; 2010).

According to a World Economic Forum report by Fan and Garcia (2019), single window systems have been adopted in 63 countries. It is observed that a range of national government bodies in charge of health, agriculture, quarantine, immigration and technical standards have integrated single window transactions. In the case of Uruguay, single window systems connect 27 agencies that are in charge of taxation, customs clearance and inspections. Moreover, they enable supply chain stakeholders to exchange 127 types of trade-related compliance documents.

Limitation of Single Window Systems

After the implementation of single window systems and the subsequent partial success stories all around the world in the 2000s and 2010s, the limitations of single window systems have started to emerge. The limitations are recognised as inter-organisational and technological issues. Even countries with the most digitised single window systems are still seeking to further reduce cross-border clearance times and gain new capabilities for cross-border trade transactions. Below are examples of such limitations, as discussed by Fan and Garcia (2019).

First, although one of the important reasons for single window implementation is process automation in cross-border transactions, it is known that full automation is not yet fully realised. This is mainly because customs payments in many countries require the importers to first pay the sum on the invoice and also to present a document to customs on site proving that the duty has been paid (e.g. in Sri Lanka). We acknowledge that the single window system was expected to play a critical role in enabling information sharing among border agencies and the private sector with increased visibility and advanced knowledge regarding incoming shipments (as discussed in the Korean single window case). However, information sharing among government bodies and private participants is still limited, especially in terms of the origin of the goods and inspection for risk management.

Information trustworthiness is also diminished when information from government and trade agencies are different from each other. Owing to the re-entry of the same data from different agencies, the trustworthiness of data in single window systems is limited. Further, owing to the misuse of corporate information by the government, the security of commercial and financial information that is submitted online is often regarded as weak. This is exacerbated in countries with limited cybersecurity protection and electronic signature laws. The critical value proposition of single window implementation is to aggregate processes into one window to enhance efficiency via data sharing and action coordination. However, many border agencies now still operate in isolation; for instance, single window systems in some Latin American countries are disconnected from customs. This is, in part, due to the legacy databases impeding the information sharing, so trade needs to deal with a 'double window'.

Blockchain Technology

Blockchain for Supply Chain Management

Blockchain refers to a set of distributed ledgers (databases) that keeps all data from transactions in a specific period time in the form of blocks through the internet or an alternative distributed network of computers. The blocks are chronologically linked and saved to all the participants' computers. The ledgers are constantly compared to each other and grow continuously to ensure all transactions are legitimate and properly recorded. Specifically, a blockchain records data in a sequential chain of cryptographic hash-linked blocks. Each block consists of a block number, the hash of the current block, the hash of the previous block within the chain, transaction records and a timestamp, as illustrated in Figure 2.3.

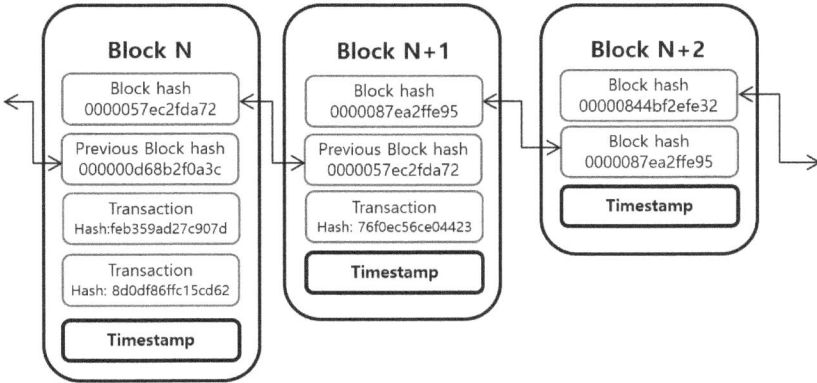

Figure 2.3: Representative structure of a blockchain. Source: Gupta (2017).

Data in each block is 'hashed' through hash functions. A hash function transforms an input (in the form of numbers and letters of any length) into an output of fixed length through a mathematical algorithm. An important characteristic of the hash function is that it is computationally impossible to use the output value to identify the original input value (in the form of numbers and letters) that was provided to the hash function. The first block is generated with a header and data. Then the subsequent block calculates its own hash using the previous block's hash. This process of adding a new block is called mining. A miner attempts to guess a number (called a *nonce*, a part of input in a hash function that is not known to the miner). If that hash is below a certain number, then a new valid block is created. The authenticity of the block is verified before it is linked to the existing chain of the blocks. The majority of the nodes in the network must agree that the new block's hash is correct and, thus, the consensus is made, and all the data in the blockchain share the same state of the data. So, to manipulate or hack the database, all the databases of all participants need to be attacked, meaning that the more participants there are, the more security is assured (Gupta 2017; Wang, Han & Beynon-Davies 2019).

Blockchain was originally thought to be dedicated only to financial market evolution, but its application is now reaching supply chain management. For example, in October 2016, IBM announced its collaboration with Walmart and Tsinghua University to digitally track and trace the movement of pork meat along its supply chain to customers across China by implementing blockchain. In 2017, IBM and Maersk were using blockchain to manage a supply chain for flower containers shipping from Kenya to the Netherlands.

Different terms are used to describe the concept of blockchain technology. Some call it a 'database' or 'distributed ledger'. Others identify it as a 'publicly verifiable open ledger', a 'distributed bookkeeping system' or a 'database containing a ledger'. These concepts highlight the blockchain's characteristic as a shared database that maintains the integrity of transactions. Although the majority of definitions highlight its data-keeping characteristics, there is a large consensus that the blockchain is a network of computers that digitises the movement of production and services (Wang, Han & Beynon-Davies 2019). The major distinction of blockchain technology from existing supply chain IT is that it enables supply chain actors to distribute and update exactly the same logical data of transactions, and it uses cryptography technology to make the transactions physically secure (Hofmann & Rüsch 2017). One can refer to Wang, Han and Beynon-Davies (2019) for more discussion regarding the role of blockchain technology for future supply chain management.

Value of Blockchain for Cross-Border Trade

Extended Traceability

Researchers have identified that blockchain technology has the capability to extend the traceability of supply chains from end to end. Centralised authority is inefficient in gathering and authorising every piece of information and transaction occurring in the web of long supply chains. Every participant has to prove themselves, and the information they provide also has to be authorised by intermediaries to ensure their accuracy. By using blockchain, such authentication is not necessary, as every node keeps its own ledgers and is updated. The traceability is also extended in terms of the completeness of information. Data in a blockchain covers information related to ownership (chronological list of owners), timestamping, location data (places the material has been, and where it is now), product-specific data (attributes and performance of the products) and environmental impact data (e.g. energy consumption, CO_2 emissions) (Abeyratne & Monfared 2016).

Metadata in a blockchain, such as price, quality, date and state of the product (e.g. locations) ensures the completeness of information and extends transparency to identify the provenance and authenticity of material and information flow (Lee & Pilkington 2017). This is also largely enabled by the time stamp. When events are ordered in the chain chronologically, each node (a header in a block) contains a field with a timestamp for when it was produced (van Engelenburg, Janssen & Klievink 2017). Thus, the nodes can be used to prove the existence of certain data before a certain time point. With this logic, the time stamp supports the management of time-sensitive issues, so revisiting the past data history is now possible (Yuan & Wang 2016). In a widely shared quote, Franck Yiannas, vice president of food safety for Walmart, noted that blockchain is a tool equivalent to FedEx for tracking the food industry (Giles 2018).

Automation Business Intelligence: Smart Contract and Amplification of IT

A *smart contract* is an agreement and also a process that can execute a part of a contract with digital verification of the stakeholders within a blockchain network (Weber & Governatori 2016). For example, if a condition from a contract is met during the process of executing a transaction, then a certain contract-based reward or action can be taken by the blockchain (e.g. cash payments). A smart contract improves the efficiency of administration by eliminating contract registration, monitoring and updating efforts and time; it establishes human trust with code trust: 'trade is settlement' (Collomb & Sok 2016). Smart contract-based business operations involve fewer manual interventions, so both manipulation risk and operational cost can be reduced. With regard to the cross-border supply chain, in 2016, Bank of America, HSBC and the Infocomm Development Authority of Singapore (IDA) declared that they had established a blockchain application based on the Hyperledger Fabric (Ganne 2018). These organisations were aiming to improve their letter of credit exchange transactions. The application followed a traditional transaction process but used a permissioned distributed ledger with a series of digital smart contracts, which allowed them to execute the deal automatically. In May 2018, HSBC announced that the 'world's first commercially viable trade finance transaction' using blockchain had been launched (Ganne 2018). The letter of credit exchange for Cargill (a US commercial group) for a movement of soya beans from Argentina to Malaysia was completed on the Voltron blockchain platform. According to Barclays bank, the letter of credit exchange process – which usually takes around seven to 10 days from issuance to approval – can be reduced to less than four hours (Fan & Garcia 2019). A smart contract solution enables supply chain partners to govern all phases of a typical trade agreement from order, shipment and invoice to final payment within a chain (Collomb & Sok 2016).

Prevention Mechanism for Data Immutability

The structure of blockchain provides a reliable information prevention mechanism for supply chain players. We can observe that the combination of immutability and peer verification plays a critical role as follows: the data in a blockchain is immutable because all the ordered sequences of transactions are saved in chronological blocks of nodes and broadcasted to all other nodes; the stored data is tamper-proof, as the majority share of the network is not compromised – updating and deleting transactions is prohibited according to the consensus mechanism (cryptographic proof with peer verification means matching the private key of a node to the public key owned by all participants; if a block is accepted, new information is added) (Weber & Governatori 2016). This is an important advancement, as it means that any falsification of the information has to be done in real time, making it so much harder a challenge than simply substituting or manipulating with new information containing different facts (Wang, Han & Beynon-Davies 2019).

The immutability of blockchain can contribute to cross-border supply chains. Implementation of mutual recognition agreements (MRA) requires information sharing among authorised economic operators (AEOs). The information sharing process is largely affected by the level of information security because of the sensitivity and confidentiality of the shared information. The shared data for the AEO is often pointed out as problematic because of lack of standards, security and integrity. The data are shared via email and Excel files containing confidential data. Blockchain technology can automate the process of AEO information sharing in a secure manner and guarantee the integrity of the information. A pilot project between Mexico and Costa Rica (CADANA) was implemented in 2018 with a common platform for the management of AEO. Based on an agreed protocol among a group of customs in different countries, each transaction was secured and protected by an immutable audit trail (Fan & Garcia 2019).

TradeLens

In January 2018, Maersk (one of the largest ocean carriers in the world) and IBM started to build a blockchain-based platform, called TradeLens, to provide a more efficient and secure way to complete cross-border trade transactions (Figure 2.4). The collaboration was originally intended in 2016 to include multiple public and private parties who would pilot the platform, including DuPont, Dow Chemical, Tetra Pak, Port Houston, Rotterdam Port Community System Portbase, the Customs Administration of the Netherlands and US Customs and Border Protection. Following a successful pilot test across several lanes in Europe and the United States in 2017, TradeLens is now operating with more than 100 participants. The parties have recorded and shared over 500 million shipping events and documents via TradeLens since its inception (White 2018).

The TradeLens blockchain is a shared, permissioned distributed ledger that records international transactions. It uses the IBM Blockchain Platform, which is based on Hyperledger Fabric, one of the Hyperledger projects hosted by the Linux Foundation, an open-source permissioned blockchain technology where the node members are captured to the supply chain network base on cryptographic identification. It enables the supply chain players to securely share copies of document filings, relevant supply chain events with shipping containers, authority approval status and audit history, so every change is transformed into a new, immutable block.

Two main capabilities have been developed to address the current challenges that cannot be fully covered by the single window system. The first is a shipping information pipeline. The blockchain-based platform provides

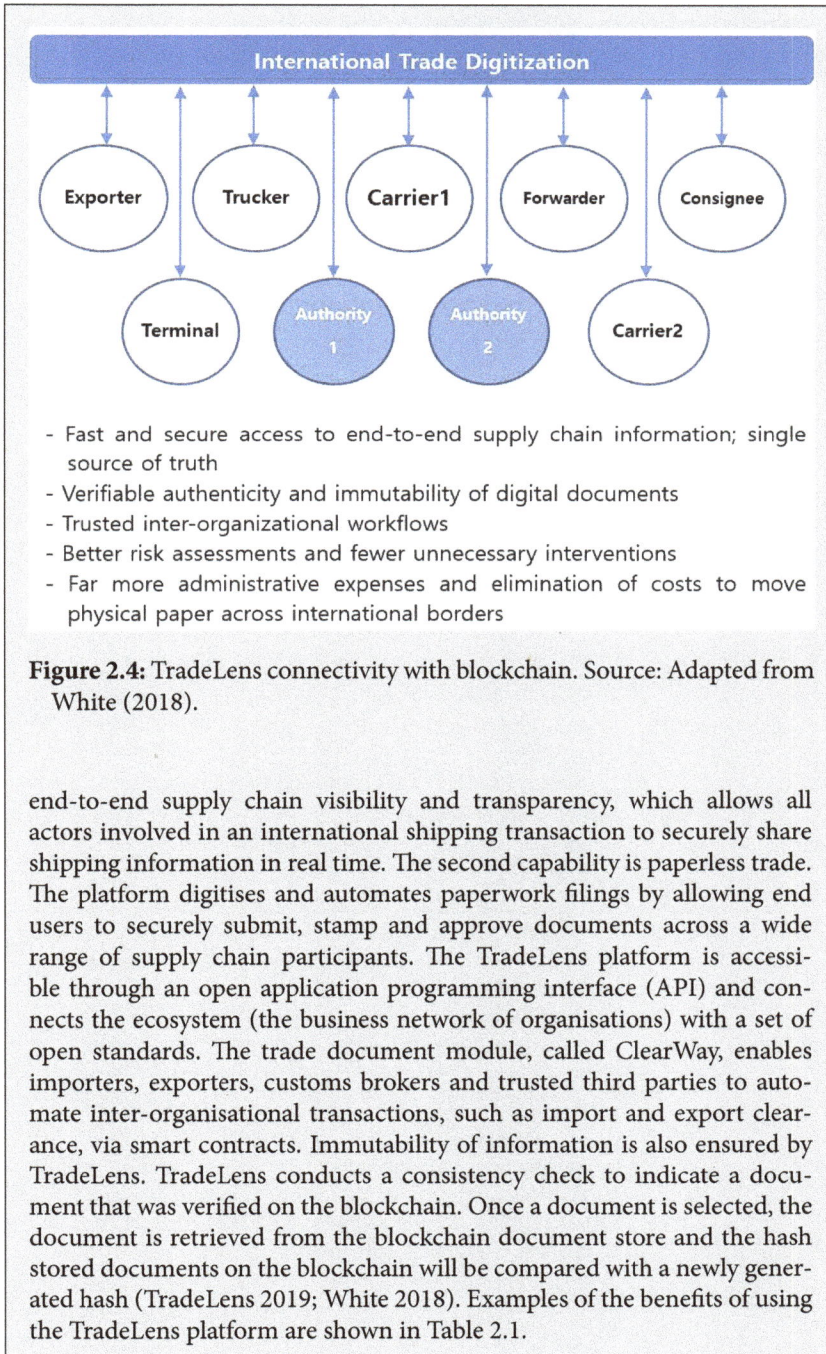

International Trade Digitization

Exporter   Trucker   Carrier1   Forwarder   Consignee

Terminal   Authority 1   Authority 2   Carrier2

- Fast and secure access to end-to-end supply chain information; single source of truth
- Verifiable authenticity and immutability of digital documents
- Trusted inter-organizational workflows
- Better risk assessments and fewer unnecessary interventions
- Far more administrative expenses and elimination of costs to move physical paper across international borders

Figure 2.4: TradeLens connectivity with blockchain. Source: Adapted from White (2018).

end-to-end supply chain visibility and transparency, which allows all actors involved in an international shipping transaction to securely share shipping information in real time. The second capability is paperless trade. The platform digitises and automates paperwork filings by allowing end users to securely submit, stamp and approve documents across a wide range of supply chain participants. The TradeLens platform is accessible through an open application programming interface (API) and connects the ecosystem (the business network of organisations) with a set of open standards. The trade document module, called ClearWay, enables importers, exporters, customs brokers and trusted third parties to automate inter-organisational transactions, such as import and export clearance, via smart contracts. Immutability of information is also ensured by TradeLens. TradeLens conducts a consistency check to indicate a document that was verified on the blockchain. Once a document is selected, the document is retrieved from the blockchain document store and the hash stored documents on the blockchain will be compared with a newly generated hash (TradeLens 2019; White 2018). Examples of the benefits of using the TradeLens platform are shown in Table 2.1.

Table 2.1: Benefits of using the TradeLens platform.

Players	Role of blockchain-based platform and possible benefits for the supply chain players
Ports and terminals	**Provide** information about the disposition of shipments within the boundaries of the port and terminal. **Benefit** from pre-built connections to shipping lines and other actors, end-to-end visibility across shipping corridors and real-time access to more information to enrich port collaboration and improve terminal planning.
Ocean carriers	**Provide** information about the disposition of shipments across the ocean leg. **Benefit** from pre-built connections to customers and ports/terminals around the world and real-time access to end-to-end supply chain events.
Customs authorities	**Provide** information about the export and import clearance status for shipments into and out of the country. **Benefit** from more informed risk assessments, better information sharing, less manual paperwork and easier connections to national single window platforms.
Freight forwarders/3PLs	**Provide** the transportation plan, inland transportation events, information on intermodal hand-off and document filings. **Benefit** from pre-built connections to the ecosystem, improved tolls for customs clearance brokerage function and real-time access to the end-to-end supply chain data to improve effectiveness of track-and-trace tools.
International transport	**Provides** information regarding the disposition of shipments carried on trucks, rail, barges, and other transportation modes. **Benefits** from improved planning and utilisation of assets (e.g. less queuing) and given real-time access to end-to-end supply chain events for shipments.
Shippers	**Engage** with the solution as a consumer of the shipping information events and paperless trade capabilities. **Benefit** from a streamlined and improved supply chain, allowing for greater predictability, early notification of issues, full transparency to validate fess and surcharges and less safety stock inventory.

Source: Adapted from White (2018).

Conclusion

Owing to the complicated process of international trade, which has intensified regulation compliance and required a wide range of intermediaries to be involved, global trade was believed to be one of the most complicated supply chain practices. The centralised platforms, namely single window platforms, were the main transactional paradigm of global e-trade solutions during the 2000s and 2010s. However, with the limitations of single window systems and the emergence of blockchain technology for the digital economy, blockchain-based, decentralised platforms in cross-border transactions are changing the paradigm of information sharing in the international setting (Table 2.2).

However, to be implemented widely, several challenges need to be resolved. One of the key technological challenges is the question of interoperability. Different types of blockchain-based platforms are being developed with different technical interfaces and algorithms that do not 'talk' to each other. Moreover, there might be resistance from current economic beneficiaries because there will always be resistance from regulators to assess the risks and incumbents who fear losing their existing revenue models. For example, with the current banking system that operates in a centralised environment, the use of this decentralised system might be a challenge, as the banks have traditionally acted as the centralised coordinator in business transactions (Michelman 2017).

From an academic perspective, to guide successful implementation of blockchain technology for cross-border supply chain management, empirical research that proves the benefits of blockchain technology should be conducted. To do so, research that identifies organisational antecedents to adopt and execute blockchain technology is required. For example, to adopt blockchain for supply chain execution, there should be an investigation of internal or external organisational conditions. Moreover, theories that support the role of blockchain technologies should be based on a robust understanding of the interface between the technology and supply chain management. For example, the resource-based view, which views IT as a competitive resource that should be confined within a firm boundary, does not justify the use of blockchain that

Table 2.2: Paradigm shift of international trade through blockchain technology.

Business model	Current	Blockchain-based
Paradigm/ architecture	Trusted third party or central coordinator	Decentralised transactions or peer-to-peer network
Database	Single copy	Peer-verified multiple copies
Security	Controlled access and firewalls	Cryptography
Transaction cost	Intermediation	Consensus and proof of work

Source: Adapted from Collomb and Sok (2016).

is actually shared by the whole actors. Moreover, there should be an effort to quantify the benefits of blockchain technology on a network or firm level that promotes the implementation of blockchain technology. In this context, the unit-of-analysis problem should be noted: in supply chain research, the majority of research uses data from a focal firm; in a blockchain context, where all of the linkages among the supply chain actors are more intensified and transparent, the unit of analysis to quantify any impact should be extended to dyadic, triadic and more.

Acknowledgement

This work was supported by an INHA UNIVERSITY research grant.

References

APEC (2007). Working towards the Implementation of Single Window within APEC Economies: Single Window Development Report. Retrieved from: https://www.apec.org/publications/2007/06/working-towards-the-imple mentation-of-single-window-within-apec-economies-single-window -development, [accessed 11 Oct 2020].

Abeyratne, S. A. & Monfared, R. P. (2016). Blockchain ready manufacturing supply chain using distributed ledger. *International Journal of Research in Engineering and Technology, 5*, 1–10. DOI: https://doi.org/10.15623/ijret .2016.0509001.

Branch, A. E. (2009). *Global supply chain management and international logistics*. Routledge.

Collomb, A. & Sok, K. (2016). Blockchain/distributed ledger technology (DLT): What impact on the financial sector? Digiworld Economic Journal, *103*, 3rd Quarter, 93–111.

Engelenburg, S. van, Janssen, M. & Klievink, B. (2017). Design of a software architecture supporting business-to-government information sharing to improve public safety and security. *Journal of Intelligent Information Systems. 52*(3), 595–618

Fan, Z. & Garcia, P. M. (2019). Windows of opportunity: Facilitating trade with blockchain technology, World Economic Forum white paper. Retrieved from: https://www.weforum.org/whitepapers/windows-of-opportunity -facilitating-trade-with-blockchain-technology [accessed 11 Oct 2020].

Ganne, E. (2018). Can blockchain revolutionize international trade? World Trade Organization. DOI: https://doi.org/10.30875/7c7e7202-en.

Giles, F. (2018). Is blockchain the future of food safety? – Growing produce. Retrieved from: https://www.growingproduce.com/fruits/blockchain-future -food-safety [accessed 27 July 2019].

Grainger, A. (2007). Supply chain security: Adding to an already complex operational and institutional environment. 2nd PICARD Conference at the World Customs, 27–28.

Gupta, M. (2017). *Blockchain for dummies*. IBM. Retrieved from: https://www-01.ibm.com/common/ssi/cgi-bin/ssialias?htmlfid=XIM12354USEN [accessed 21 March 2018].

Hofmann, E. & Rüsch, M. (2017). Industry 4.0 and the current status as well as future prospects on logistics. *Computers in Industry, 89*, 23–34. DOI: https://doi.org/10.1016/j.compind.2017.04.002.

Lee, J. H. & Pilkington, M. (2017). How the blockchain revolution will reshape the consumer electronics industry. *IEEE Consumer Electronics Magazine, 6*, 19–23. DOI: https://doi.org/10.1109/MCE.2017.2684916.

Michelman, P. (2017). Seeing beyond the blockchain hype. *MIT Sloan Management Review, 58*, 17–19.

Microsoft. (2017). How blockchain will transform the modern supply chain. Retrieved from: https://azure.microsoft.com/mediahandler/files/resource files/how-blockchain-will-transform-modern-supply-chain/how-block chain-will-transform-modern-supply-chain.pdf [accessed 27 July 2019].

TradeLens (2019). TradeLens solution brief – edition two, Retrieved from https://www.maersk.com/local-information/west-central-asia/india/local -solutions/tradelens-connects, date accessed 5 January 2020.

UNECE (2010). Republic of Korea single window case. Retrieved from: https://www.unece.org/fileadmin/DAM/cefact/single_window/sw_cases/Down load/Korea_Customs.pdf [accessed 27 July 2019].

UNECE (2011). Republic of Korea. Retrieved from: http://www.unece.org/fileadmin/DAM/cefact/single_window/sw_cases/Download/Republic ofKorea.pdf [accessed 27 July 2019].

UNECE (2019). The single window concept. Retrieved from: http://tfig.unece .org/contents/single-window-for-trade.htm [accessed 27 July 2019].

Wang, Y., Han, J. H. & Beynon-Davies, P. (2019). Understanding blockchain technology for future supply chains: A systematic literature review and research agenda. *Supply Chain Management*. DOI: https://doi.org/10.1108 /SCM-03-2018-0148.

Weber, I. & Governatori, G. (2016). Untrusted business process monitoring and execution using blockchain. International Conference on Business Process Management, 329–347. DOI: https://doi.org/10.1007/978-3-319-45348-4.

White, M. (2018). Digitizing global trade with Maersk and IBM – blockchain pulse: IBM Blockchain Blog. Retrieved from: https://www.ibm.com/blogs /blockchain/2018/01/digitizing-global-trade-maersk-ibm [accessed 27 July 2019].

Yuan, Y. & Wang, F. Y. (2016). Towards blockchain-based intelligent transportation systems. 19th International Conference on Intelligent Transportation Systems, 2663–2668. DOI: https://doi.org/10.1109/ITSC.2016.7795984.

CHAPTER 3

Leveraging AI for Asset and Inventory Optimisation

Sid Shakya, Anne Liret and Gilbert Owusu

Introduction

Service organisations are typified by resources, both human and non-human. Human resources comprise the front and back office staff, and non-human resources include spares, network assets etc. Managing resources to meet customer demands is one of the key challenges in any large service organisations. It is well recognised that the proactive management of resources is one of the key contributors to the performance and profitability of service organisations (Shakya et al. 2013). Proactive resource management provides the framework to optimise the cost and quality of the products and services an organisation offers. It is one of many challenges that service organisations are faced with on a regular basis. There are, for example, specific challenges to be tackled in resource management, such as making decisions on many different types of resources that a company should maintain, and, more importantly, on managing the ways these different resources interact together to create products and service (Owusu & O'Brien 2013; Shakya et al. 2017).

A case in point is that fixing broadband at a customer's premises may involve a field technician, a vehicle, spare parts, a call centre operator and the network.

How to cite this book chapter:
Shakya, S., Liret, A., and Owusu, G. 2022. Leveraging AI for Asset and Inventory Optimisation. In: Wang, Y., and Pettit, S. (eds.) *Digital Supply Chain Transformation: Emerging Technologies for Sustainable Growth*. Pp. 39–60. Cardiff: Cardiff University Press. DOI: https://doi.org/10.18573/book8.c. Licence: CC-BY-NC-ND 4.0

These are all classified as resources. Each of these resources can have different capabilities (i.e. functions), capacity and/or a geographical requirement. For example, a specific field engineer may have broadband installation skills and plumbing skills, whereas another field engineer may have cable and fibre jointing skills. Similarly, a vehicle type could be a van with light equipment or it could be a truck that is able to carry large heavy equipment. This also applies to spare parts, call centre operators, or network services with various capabilities and different specifications, which may lead to many possible variations of service offerings. Managing these diverse resources to support the efficient delivery of products and services is a crucial and challenging problem.

In recent years, there has been a strong drive to leverage best practice in the supply chain management domain to service operations (Voudouris 2008). Recent research has shown that this increasingly involves the automation of planning processes (Owusu et al. 2013). The key objective of planning is to have the right resource available at the right time in the right place to fulfil customer demand. Advanced planning of resources helps firms to maximise utilisation and minimise waste, and by doing so it also helps firms to fulfil customer demands and maximise revenue, while minimising cost. One of the key prerequisites for successful planning is the optimal deployment of strategic resources to enable a frictionless delivery service.

In this chapter we deal with assets and inventories, one of the key resources that service organisations such as telecommunications and utility companies maintain. There are two dimensions – *strategic* and *operational* – to the deployment challenge. The strategic dimension focuses on deploying fixed assets to ensure that the organisation is set up for optimal performance. The operational dimension focuses on replenishing inventories (spares) for efficient delivery of services in alignment with service level agreements with customers (SLA). As with any other resource types, the timely availability of spare parts can have a positive impact on service quality. Therefore, it is very important to have the right spares in the right place and at the right time. Spare parts are normally kept in warehouses or distribution centres. It is therefore very important that the warehouses are also built in the right places, where they can provide the maximum value to the organisation while minimising the travel time and maximising the distribution coverage. This is a combinatorial optimisation problem. Real-world combinatorial optimisation problems involve a heterogeneous set of side constraints (i.e. rules). Modelling and maintaining such rules or constraints is non-trivial for complex problems. Operational requirements such as reuse and model configurability make AI (in particular heuristic search methods) a prime candidate for solving combinatorial optimisation problems for operational use.

The remainder of the chapter is structured as follows. The next section focuses on using AI to model and solve the challenge of strategically deploying assets. In the subsequent section, we focus on the replenishment of spares. We provide use cases to give insight into how we operationalised these models.

Strategic Deployment of Assets – the IoT
and Inventory Management

Recent advancement in the IoT (internet of things) and connected technologies have had an impact on how warehouses are built and managed. Increasingly, warehouses are getting smaller and mobile in their nature, shifting from fixed structures, such as brick-and-mortar buildings, to mobile containers or even lockers. They are remotely monitored and operated, and the right to access is normally given on demand, accessible with a programmed device or unique passcode that is generated per visit. A fixed number of personnel (typically engineers and technicians) are assigned to these mobile warehouses based on their home locations and working locations, such that the distances they need to travel to get spares and get to the clients or repair sites are minimised. These mobile warehouses can be quickly deployed to different locations in a very short time. More importantly, they can be moved from one location to another and can be redeployed and reused, if required.

A typical case of redeployment in a telecom scenario would be that the demand for service at a certain location need to be shifted to another location because of the completion of a new housing project, which leads to the completion of the telecom infrastructure deployment in that area. In such a case, the mobile storage facilities near to the area can be relocated to a new area where a new project has started. Another example would be a situation where fewer repair jobs are required in certain areas and therefore spare parts are not required as frequently as in the past. This may be due to a change in technology or an upgrade to the telecom infrastructure. In such cases, the mobile warehouses can be moved to areas where they could be better utilised. Furthermore, in some cases, mobile warehouses are used by several lines of business (LoBs) simultaneously, both within the same organisation or contracted to an external organisation. There could be a complex SLA (service level agreement) with specifications such as who can use the mobile warehouses and how/when they can be used, typically operated through a booking system. A case for redeployment happens when a new LoB or new organisation is added in the service chain to use the mobile warehouses. In many cases, a new set of mobile warehouses would require a fresh deployment. This also occurs when an organisation leaves the service chain.

The location where these mobile warehouses can be deployed can also have constraints, such as the availability of a fenced perimeter, accessible by a large vehicle delivering spare parts, and a requirement for electricity. Therefore, certain locations are pre-determined as suitable hosting sites. The task then becomes finding the best location out of the suitable locations set to deploy or redeploy the mobile warehouses.

The problem is trivial if fewer mobile warehouses are involved with a small number of users and sites. The deployment decision could be made manually and accurately. However, this is not the case with most large service organisations. They can have hundreds of such mobile warehouses serving thousands of engineers with thousands of possible deployment locations to choose from. In such scenarios, a manual design of the deployment locations of mobile warehouses can be prohibitively time-consuming. More importantly, the design can be sub-optimal in terms of the distribution coverage and travel time required by engineers to acquire the spare parts.

A Use Case at BT

BT operates a large network infrastructure in the UK. It has over 22,000 field engineers maintaining over 5,000 exchanges, serving millions of customers and supporting many products and services. It uses a huge inventory and thousands of spare parts per day to repair or upgrade the network equipment, both at customer premises and at exchange buildings. The technicians travel to warehouses each morning to source the spare parts that they require to perform the tasks assigned to them for that day. Some parts could be specific to a task; others could be general spares such as cables and sockets. Keeping the correct number of spare parts in each warehouse is crucial for field operations. Furthermore, specialised spare parts sourced for a specific task should be delivered to the warehouse in a timely manner to complete the task in time and not to miss other impending appointments.

BT operates over 90 fixed warehouses and distribution centres across the UK where engineers can collect spare parts that they have ordered. Engineers travel routinely, sometimes more than once a day, to get the parts that they require. Fixed warehouse locations can cause some issues such as long travel times, particularly when the home location of the engineer is far from the warehouse, and more often when the site where the task has to be done is also far from the warehouse. In addition, those sites currently serve tasks at over 5,000 exchanges across the country. To increase efficiency, BT wants to increase the number of warehouses operational in the country from 90 to over 700 to minimise travel. Furthermore, those new warehouses will be mobile, capable of being quickly deployed and redeployed as and when needed. The new mobile warehouses would keep a set of small storage spaces, or lockers. Each of the lockers can keep parts required by a specific technician. Spare parts would be delivered to the locker as per the booking made, sometimes couriered for a rapid delivery. A technician would get fixed or one-time credentials to access the locker.

The lockers would be hosted at BT's exchange sites, which are capable of handling large delivery trucks, and with a fenced perimeter. However, finding the best 700 exchanges out of 5,000 possible exchanges to host the mobile warehouses is a difficult task, especially when they have to be redeployed every few months. Warehouses have to be deployed in such a way that:

1. The cumulative expected travel time for all technicians across the country is minimised.
2. The differences in distance from a warehouse to the served exchange sites should be minimal, to avoid long travel times to certain sites.

3. The differences in distance from a warehouse to the home locations of the assigned technicians should be minimised, to avoid cases where some technicians travel very short distances while others travel long distances.
4. The differences in the number of the tasks that warehouses are expected to serve per day should be minimal. This is to avoid a situation where some warehouses are extremely busy serving many tasks compared with other warehouses.
5. The differences in the numbers of technicians that the warehouses serve should be minimal. This is for the same reason for the case above.

Warehouse Deployment as an Optimisation Problem

Organisations are increasingly looking to AI techniques to solve large-scale industrial problems. They have been proven to provide good solutions for many real-world problems. Latest advancements in machine learning and deep data mining, and their successful application in some cutting-edge inventions such as self-driving cars, drones and augmented and virtual realities, has further highlighted the effectiveness of AI techniques, with organisations increasingly moving to adopt such techniques in their decision-making process.

The five conditions mentioned in the previous section can be considered the objectives of the warehouse deployment problem and the problem itself can be modelled as a combinatorial optimisation problem, where the goal is to find the 700 best locations out of 5,000 possible locations that satisfy the above objectives.

A manual approach to solving the same problem would involve a set of heuristics to find the 700 initial sites, evaluating them and manually exchanging sites to see if there is any improvement on the objectives. However, this would be very time-consuming, given the combinatorial nature of the problem. This is where AI techniques can be useful.

In the following sections it is briefly shown how the problem is modelled as an optimisation problem and how AI techniques are being used to solve this problem.

AI Approach to Solving the Problem

A simple greedy logic (GL) heuristic for solving the problem would be to choose n sites with a large number of tasks as the initial warehouse locations. Then create n cluster of sites by assigning all the remaining sites to the warehouse sites based on nearest distance. Evaluate the warehouse sites by calculating values for each of the five objectives and adding them together to get a weighted combined objective value. This objective value is sometimes known as solution fitness value. Then iteratively move to better deployment by changing a warehouse location to a neighbouring site one by one and accepting the new deployment if the combined objective is better.

The core idea of the heuristic here is that choosing the sites with large numbers of tasks as the initial warehouse location is likely to minimise the travel
time. The motivation here is that the tasks for those initial warehouses will
not require any travel. This, however, could conflict with other objectives. For
example, minimising the travel time may not minimise the differences among
the travel distances between sites. It may be that some sites require long travel
times while others may require very short travel times, even though cumulative
travel time may be minimal, resulting in the preference being given to one set
of sites at the expense of others. In the optimisation literature, this type of solution is termed the local optimal solution.

A more sophisticated approach would be to use advanced search heuristics
such as a genetic algorithm (GA) to optimise the warehouse allocation problem. GAs are a class of population-based evolutionary algorithms (Goldberg
1989) that find solutions for problems using the concept of natural selection
and recombination to evolve a better solution (Larrañaga & Lozano 2002;
Shakya & Santana 2012). One of the core strengths of GAs is the way they represent solutions (Goldberg 1989).

The obvious approach for this problem is to represent each deployment $x =$
$\{x_1, x_2 \dots x_n\}$ as a GA solution, where each x_I, which is the chosen exchange for
deployment of warehouse I, is considered as a solution variable.

The next component of a GA is defined as the fitness, $f(x)$, of a given solution
x, representing the quality of the solution. In this case, the combined objective
value of five objectives for a solution x is used as the fitness value for solution x. The objective for the GA is then to find the best values for solution x
such that fitness $f(x)$ is minimised. This optimisation task can be expressed as
below (eq. 1):

$$\min_{x = \{x_1, x_2, \dots x_n\}} f(x) = \alpha Trv(x) + \beta \Delta Tsk(x) + \gamma \Delta Tch(x) \tag{1}$$

Here, $Trv(x)$ represents the first three objectives, related to travel. represents
objective 4, related to difference in task, and $\Delta Tch(x)$ represents objective 5,
related to difference in served technicians. Given a solution x, it is trivial to
calculate values for each of these three terminologies. The parameters α, β and
γ are the weights applied to the respective terms. This provides explicit control
over which of the objectives to be prioritised as per the requirements of the
design in different scenarios.

Unlike traditional methods, where an algorithm works directly with the problem definition, GAs try to evolve the solution by working with the population of
solutions as a whole and selecting the better solution while letting worse solutions
die off over multiple generations, so as to increase the density of good solutions in
the population and recombining them to create even better solutions.

The difference between GAs and the greedy logic (GL) is that GL works with
a single solution and tries to find the best locations by assuming that assigning the sites with high volumes of tasks as warehouses are likely to minimise

the travel time, thus not properly considering other objectives. In contrast, GAs continue to evolve to find the best locations that balance all the objectives against one another and explore a wider part of the search space by working with multiple solutions at once.

Business Impact

The AI logic described in the previous section was incorporated into a tool called Intuitu strategic planner (Figures 3.1 and 3.2), which is being used by BT to plan the mobile warehouse deployment. In Figure 3.2, each central node

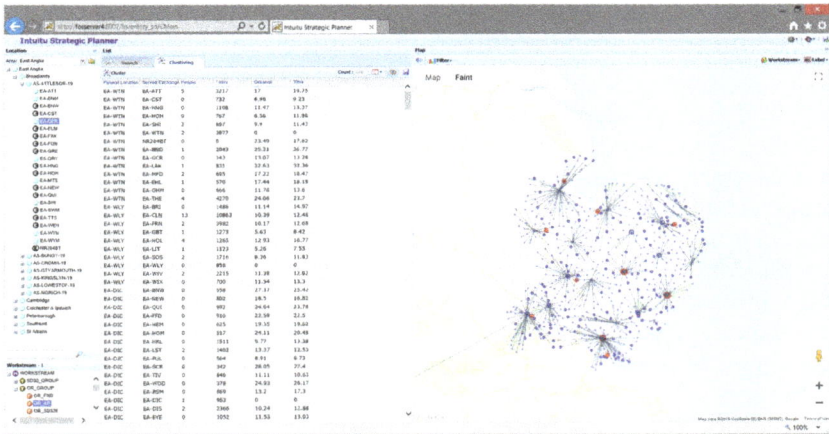

Figure 3.1: Intuitu Strategic Planner tool.

Figure 3.2: A design by Intuitu for 600 locations.

represents a proposed warehouse location and each edge pointing to the central node represents a site that is served by the central node. Our approach has made noticeable improvements for the business in terms of the cost savings due to reduced deployment time and reduced travel time for technicians to source spare parts and to perform tasks assigned to them with increased SLAs.

The combined value of the benefits by the project over a five-year period is estimated to be millions of pounds in cost savings due to a reduction in deployment travel time for technicians. Other benefits include improving the quality of the decision-making process by enabling what-if scenario modelling.

A Use Case of Operational Replenishment of Inventories and Assets

In the previous section we saw a use case of the strategic dimension to inventory and asset management, which focused on the strategic deployment of warehouses to ensure that the organisation is set up for optimal performance. In this section we present a second use case. The focus is on the operational aspect of inventory management. As mentioned before, the operational dimension to inventory management is about replenishing inventories (spares) for the efficient delivery of services in alignment with the agreed service level agreed with customers (SLA).

A typical operational journey starts with a demand linked to a fault at a client site impacting one or multiple parts (pieces of asset). This demand is associated with a service assurance that constrains the faulty part to being repaired within a pre-agreed time, which could vary from two weeks down to less than one day. Once the fault is identified and the availability of the relevant spare part has been confirmed, a job is created and assigned to a field technician for further survey and fixing operation. When a part is picked up by the engineer out of a warehouse stock, there is an update process over the supply chain, to ensure any future task allocation decision takes into account the remaining volume of accurate spares. Figure 3.3 outlines the typical flow of operations in an organisation responsible for asset-constrained service of maintenance.

It is well recognised that it is possible to apply AI reasoning to recommend a proactive decision for the transfer of spares to the warehouses according to configurable asset management policies, while optimising the overall cost such as storage of asset and shipping taxes (Desport et al. 2016). The use case here was to build a plan of asset transfer between warehouses over a given number of days and compare the plan against different asset replenishment policies and demand profile. Such decisions are typically made to address the asset replenishment problem. When the same asset is common across the business or can be used to serve different clients, the asset management includes:

1. an estimate of how many and where/for which client the asset will need to be replaced;

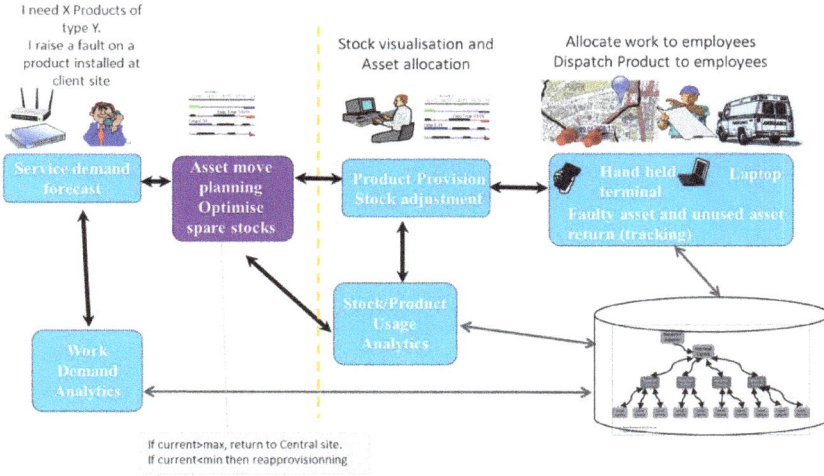

Figure 3.3: AI-supported asset-constrained service flow.

2. an evaluation of the optimum volume of spare stock of such pooled assets that allows the customer needs to be served under the agreed commitments;
3. what policy for the replenishment of those assets is recommended according to the criticality of customer contract or the asset cost.

In the telecommunications, facilities and energy sectors, maintenance service providers have to address the large-scale real-world variants of asset management across multiple customers and over a distribution network of widespread stock warehouses and repair centres. A typical distribution network in e-logistics is composed of a repairer or supplier node, a main national centre, regional centres dependent on the national centre, and a set of local centres dependent on the regional centres. The topology of the network defines the allowance and cost of asset transfer between two nodes of the network (i.e. two centres). When a new or repaired asset comes into the chain, the process moves it from supplier node down to one of the suitable centres. When a faulty asset is returned to the repair centre, the process moves it from local centres to the repairer.

A Typical Use Case

As a case in point, a maintenance agreement of premium service assurance can require a full fix within four to eight hours, which means all the following steps have to be completed within that time range:

1. assigning a field technician,
2. collecting the spare part at the warehouse,

3. travelling to the client site, and
4. replacing the faulty part.

It is well known that the field force scheduling aspect of the problem only can be operationally automated and enhanced using a vehicle routing problem model and heuristic search solution approach (Liret 2008). Nevertheless, the problem variant with asset collection at warehouse and completion in very short response time requirement is a challenge to performing optimally. As a matter of fact, field engineers could not have time to collect spares, travel and perform the job unless a spare is present in the nearest warehouse. More precisely, to solve this problem, a proactive planning solution is needed to plan a minimum number of spares ahead so that, operationally, there is sufficient relevant spares in place at the nearest warehouse to the client site. The volume of spares to plan is inherently a function of an acceptable business risk, usually estimated by services assurance management teams and supply chain operations teams.

There is thus a proactive replenishment planning problem to solve in order to transfer the right amount of the right spare asset in alignment with the service assurance. To solve that problem in a sustainable manner, one needs a hybrid approach towards the asset movement planning in order to optimally meet the service assurance across as many client sites as possible, while recommending the risk of shortages for the warehouse and service contracts. When a fault profile is predicted (based on client, asset features and geography), the approach would extend to targeting any required replenishment action (asset transfer) ahead of the fault estimated date. The assumption in this section is that assets can be used across multiple clients and countries. Thus, the question is how to optimise the storage of these assets for seamless reuse.

Whereas the strategic aspect of mobile warehouse deployment supports the right positioning of warehouse of assets for service assurance, the operational aspect of asset transfer plans supports the decisions over which product and which spare volume should be replenished (i.e. transferred) at which warehouse (mobile or fixed). In both cases, IoT technologies are key enablers of a zero-touch approach across the service chain.

Asset Move for Automated Replenishment Supported by the IoT

As mentioned in previous use case, the IoT is changing the way businesses maintain equipment, write service agreements and set customer expectations in the process – i.e. exploring a new approach to maintenance that is driven by insights, instead of errors. Today, most companies offer scheduled maintenance as part of an equipment service contract. The IoT now enables a shift from just consuming data from connected devices to gaining visibility into the current state of equipment and using that information to deliver a different type of field service while operating the inventory and asset network in a more proactive manner. We can now use data from sensors that indicate an asset's health to act based on the probability of a fault occurrence. It has been suggested that the IoT will shortly enable businesses to shift from recurring preventative maintenance plans to the proactive monitoring of devices and predictive maintenance (Pintov & Brandeleer 2019). Indeed, IoT platforms can host artificial intelligence (AI) components that monitor trends and predict which installed asset is likely to fail. AI and data science provide the ability to process massive amounts of information (given the right dataset), which help to inform the need for increasing the volume of spares in particular warehouse at certain date.

This kind of reasoning will reduce the likelihood of maintenance delays while improving customer satisfaction. This approach, however, poses a number of challenges. For client service assurance management, we want to ensure the SLA can always be met on existing maintenance contracts, with a recommended risk of reaching a shortage in spares in the event that a new client site or contract is evaluated.

There are number of questions that have to be answered:

1. According to a risk function, do we have enough spare to cover short SLA contracts? Are they at the right locations? If not, how much time will it take to get the right coverage?
2. Do we have enough equipment in stock at the right locations to cover contract requirements? If not, can we recommend actions (plan of asset move, invest in new asset) to meet the short SLA service assurance?
3. Do we have stock in surplus, i.e. assets that are not used nor related to any potential contract?
4. Knowing a demand profile, what is the most suitable asset decision that de-risks the service (i.e. minimises the volume of unmet demand or penalties)?
5. What acceptable risk rate can we afford with a given stock and client sites scenario without investing? What is the best risk rate to apply for a given client, product or geographical area, knowing the reported faults, proactive asset moves, and risk rate used in the past?

The high-level problem could be outlined as in Figure 3.4. The functional component is notified by a number of inputs such as a change in the customer sites and warehouses –which could be represented by an address and a capacity of installed or stored parts, and a distribution network linking these sites according to some policy of transfer. Moreover, to be able to analyse the state of equipment and estimate their fault likelihood, a certain level of accuracy in the volume of spares (different status) in addition to a certain agility in updating the real-time data is expected. Another key input is the model for penalties and client priorities.

The output of a typical asset replenishment process would be a plan over a number of days recommending a set of transfers of assets from the warehouse to other locations closer to the client site, while minimising the overall cost

Inputs   Outputs

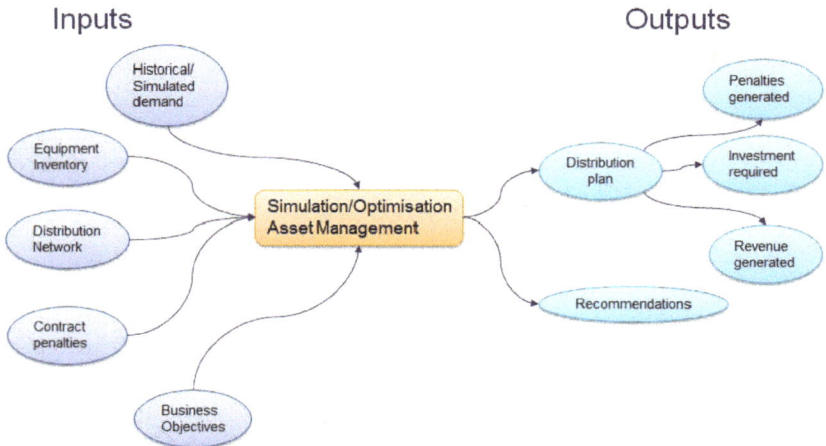

Figure 3.4: Problem statement.

(storage, transfer, penalty fees) and assessing the asset products that are estimated to be at risk (since there are installed occurrences not covered by a spare
one), and some recommendations for investing in critical assets.

Replenishment Optimisation Problem

Desport et al. (2016; 2017; 2019) proposed a heuristic search-based model
optimising the planning of asset volumes at each location of a list of sites, in
closed-loop chains, taking into account a pre-known demand, unit costs for transferring part from one location to another one, and unit costs for storing the assets.
This model addresses the pure asset move problem. Asset move planning covers
only one part of the replenishment problem (the reusable one in a closed loop).
However, to apply this approach to real-word, client-wise costs, service assurance
risk estimates and some equivalence knowledge reasoning between reusable products are required. Introducing these features into the asset move planning problem
allows us to assess the benefits of an augmented AI-based automated supply chain
decision, which has traditionally been made by human and most frequently driven
with a siloed view of each client's product needs. We use AI to gain flexibility
in decision-making and recommendation against uncertain and dynamic demand
trends in assets (fault prediction and asset provisioning due to contract).

We propose a hybrid AI simulation approach with the aim of de-risking
asset decisions for customer service. We model the problem as an extension of
Desport et al. (2017):

1. In addition to the demand profile, a *minimum spare stock amount* per
   client contract is defined according to a service assurance policy and an
   acceptable risk rule. The risk value is defined as a rule for a given product,

and minimum stock level as a function of risk value, the spare for the product in each warehouse, and the SLA of contract on the same product. For instance, a simple risk rule is: '1 spare is required for 10 installed parts at client site', '2 spares for 11 to 20 installed parts', etc. If two client sites are mapped to a city node (e.g. PARIS), one client having 32 CLK routers installed and another client 14 CLK routers installed, then the minimum stock of CLK product for node PARIS will be 1+ (46 modulo 10), i.e. five spare pieces of CLK product.

2. The client's priority is defined as a cost of penalty if a service is not covered as per the minimum stock constraint defined in (1); for any potentially missing spare, a risk is estimated, and a penalty cost defined.

   1. Cost incurred when a delay in service occurs: this penalty can be, for instance, a function of contractual fixed fees for each day of delay, and of a variable component function of the unit penalty per product and day of delay, and of the number of assets estimated at risk because not covered by a spare at nearest warehouse node. Both components can be weighted by a product-wise or customer-wise factor.

   2. Cost of healthy/faulty storage, function of (asset, node): each asset stored in a warehouse will incur a cost, which is configurable per product and warehouse node.

   3. Cost of not reaching the minimum stock for any tuple (node, product): a cost will be incurred on a daily basis if the latter is not satisfied.

   4. Cost of shipping a number of products during a transfer function of (origin, destination, asset): any valid move will incur a transfer cost (which could be zero, for instance when bringing an asset back to the main repair centre).

   5. Cost of repairing an asset or sending it to the manufacturer, function of (asset).

3. Valued topology of distribution network: each warehouse (depot) and customer site is abstracted as a node of an oriented network. Depots can be of various superficies and storage can cost vary depending on the region. In the problem model, tuning the storage cost allows us to iteratively identify the suitable policy of storage. For instance, if assets from the same product are installed on different clients based in different cities all in the same region, there is a choice between storing spares at the regional warehouse or distributing the spares in smaller volumes in each city local warehouse. The level of service assurance as well as the transfer cost influences this decision.

4. Handling faulty parts: in a supply chain, faulty assets are transferred back to the repair centre either internally to provider, or directly to the manufacturer with the target that after a period of time a healthy asset can be reinjected into the chain (closed-loop supply chain). With the support of the IoT, we can imagine an automated approach that allows triggering the transfer back and the reinjection of a given product in a given warehouse.

AI Approach to Solving the Problem

The problem can be modelled as a constrained optimisation problem (Hooker 2012; Taleizadeh, Niaki & Aryanezhad 2010), where decision variables represent possible actions, a set of constraints allows business rules to be represented, and a list of costs items is to be minimised. Basing the solving algorithm on AI techniques known as meta-heuristics, an iterative process is considering suitable moves (partial valuing of the solution) and performing the best moves in the search space. For each valid move (satisfying the constraints), the impact on the costs is computed and then, depending on the meta-heuristic strategy chosen, the move will be accepted or rejected. Moves in this problem can be any of the following:

1. bringing in new asset using available capital expenditure (CAPEX),
2. moving assets between different storage warehouses, and
3. repairing assets and reinjecting them into the network.

The strategy chosen in this use case is based on a heuristic search applying a best improvement neighbourhood selection: each feasible move represents the transfer of a volume of asset from one node to another node in the distribution network. Each transfer incurs a cost and an update of the volume at each impacted node. The transfer is validated by the heuristic search only if it leads to a cost improvement that reduces the overall penalty cost across all clients, while limiting the storage and transfer cost. Thus, the volume of transfer will be bundled (grouped) to avoid extra transfer cost. Further, the asset will not be moved if an equivalent product is already in place in sufficient volume. The latter approach requires the modelling of an equivalent model between products and its incorporation into the risk rule and minimum stock evaluation. With regard to constraints, a constraints network restricts the list of valid asset moves and actions considered by the algorithm; from the topology of the distribution network, a set of constraints defines valid transfers (oriented) between centres along with their duration, and status of assets (healthy or faulty) and type of product (heavy or not). This is important to reflect organisational policy (faulty parts are to reach a repair centre, for instance), as well as allowing sufficient agility in the adjustment of the topology without invalidating the replenishment optimisation method.

Business Impact

The output of such optimisation and AI-driven tool includes:

1. asset moves plan 1–7 days (all involved in a four-hour SLA) (plus estimated reduction for financial risk as impact) to cover service assurance with existing spares in supply chain, as outlined in Figure 3.5;

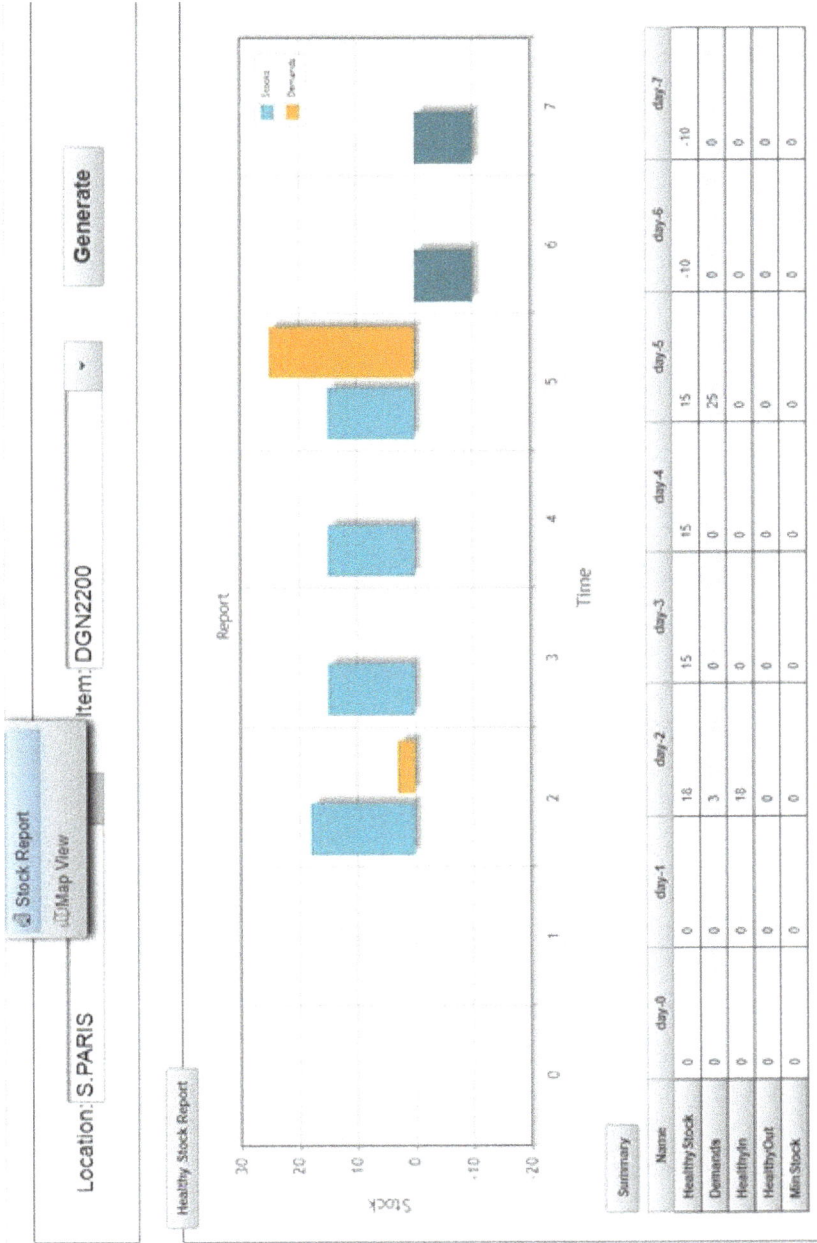

Figure 3.5: Example of report dashboard of recommended asset transfer plan.

Name	day-0	day-1	day-2	day-3	day-4	day-5	day-6	day-7
Healthy Stock	0	0	18	15	15	15	-10	-10
Demands	0	0	3	0	0	25	0	0
HealthyIn	0	0	18	0	0	0	0	0
HealthyOut	0	0	0	0	0	0	0	0
MinStock	0	0	0	0	0	0	0	0

Node	Product Id	Nb Equipm under Contract	minimum stock	Stock Before	Stock After
S.PARIS	PWR-2700-AC/4	2	45	0	6
S.PARIS	GLC-T690	1	30	0	11
S.PARIS	7600-MRSFC/4	1	31	1	10
S.PARIS	WS-F6700-CFC	1	36	3	30
S.PARIS	WS-X6724-SFP-D	1	23	0	23
S.PARIS	PWR-MX904-AC-S	2	22	0	0
S.PARIS	FAN-MOD-4HS	1	22	5	10
S.PARIS	CISCO3x7604	1	19	2	5
S.PARIS	CWDM-SFP-1490	2	17	3	3
S.PARIS	RE-MX-104	1	11	0	0
S.PARIS	MX104-AJX5-AC	1	11	1	1
S.PARIS	7600-PWR-C/3C-10GGE	1	10	0	0
S.PARIS	MIC-3D-20GE-SFP-E	1	10	1	1
S.PARIS	MEM-XCEF720-256M	1	11	2	2
S.PARIS	RSPP20-SC-10GE	1	8	8	3
S.PARIS	FANTRAY-MX104-S	1	11	3	3
S.PARIS	X2-10GB-LR	2	6	0	6
S.PARIS	C9xxB-48T	4	1	0	0

Figure 3.6: Result of risk on products and asset replenishment recommendation.

Table 3.1: Example of service de-risking impact following asset move plan deployment.

ODE ID	Product	Min-Stock	Stock of spares before	Stock of spares after	unmet 4 hours SLA before optimisation	unmet 4 hours SLA after optimisation
WH.RENNES	CLK-7600	1	2	1	1	0
WH.STRASBG	CLK-7600	1	0	1	−1	0
WH.PARIS	CLK-7600	6	0	6	−6	0
WH.ORLEANS	CLK-7600	1	0	1	−1	0
WH.LILLE	CLK-7600	1	0	1	−1	0

2. recommendation of equipment/contract at risk (not covered), as in Figure 3.6;
3. recommendation of a site or warehouse nodes, contract, or asset where an action is needed such as purchase, resell or move;
4. recommendation on stock not primarily used (could inform about the feasibility of engaging a new contract within an existing mutualised pot of spares);
5. review of stock and client sites alignment through a geographical view (map), identifying shortage, risk and surplus before and after optimisation (Table 3.1).

Figure 3.5 outlines the qualitative and quantitative impacts that asset move automated planning and processing could provide. Impact can be observed at various levels:

1. *Healthy Stock*: evolution of healthy stock throughout time horizon (negative value reflects non-met demand);
2. *Demand*: number of assets requested on that particular day;
3. *Healthy In*: number of healthy assets received on that day;
4. *Healthy Out*: number of healthy assets lost (due to demand or external move);
5. *MinStock*: minimum stock required for that asset on that day.

Figure 3.5 illustrates a plan over seven days from the perspective of a local warehouse in one large city. On day 2, the PARIS warehouse has received 18 new DGN2200 assets and has a demand for three of those assets. On day 3, we can see that the demand was reduced from the stock, leaving 15 assets left. Starting day 2 with a stock of 20 spares, from day 6, as a result of two peaks of demand, the warehouse is missing 10 spares to serve the total demand over this week's period. This example typically shows the kind of risky situation that could happen when replenishment and provisioning is not planned against a proper service demand profile.

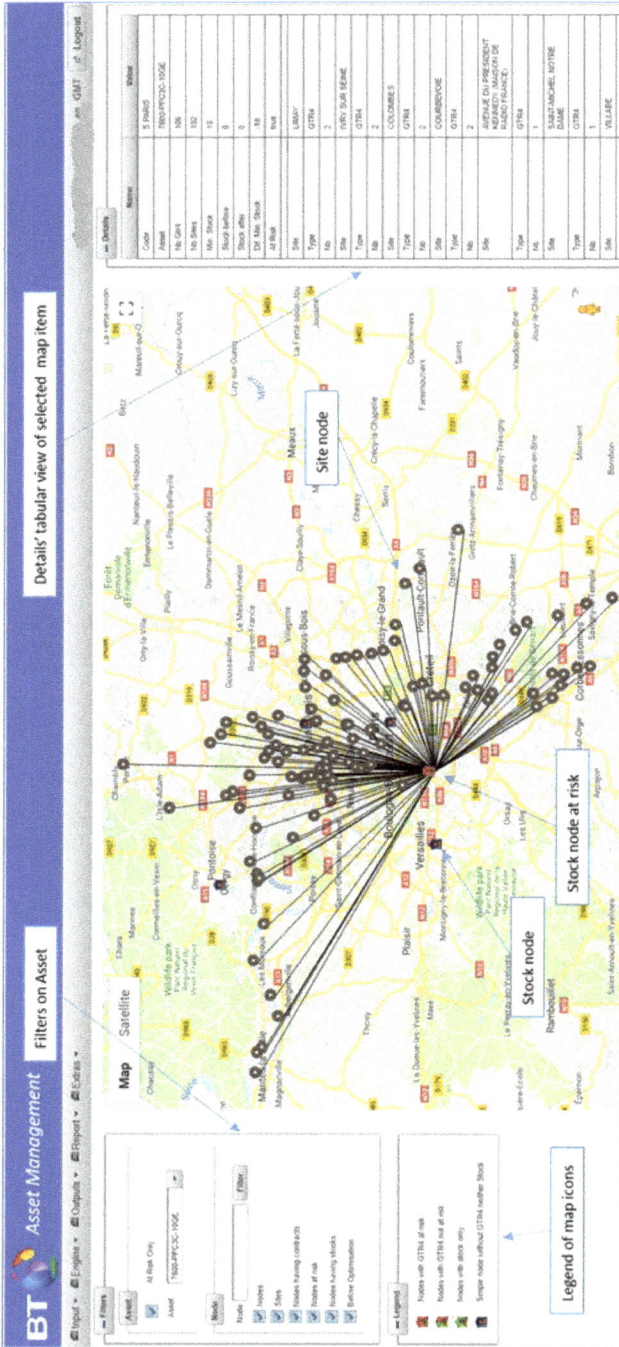

Figure 3.7: Map from one depot for asset 7600-PFC3C-10GE.

On the other hand, when asset move plan has been followed, as in the example of Table 3.1 below, the risk was initially highlighted for product CLK-7600 – the volume of uncovered installed asset before optimisation – which is represented by the value of '*unmet 4 hours SLA before*'. This value is negative, which means that some spares are missing and the risk of the installed asset is not entirely covered by the service. The risk is then reduced to the point of having no contract at risk after the deployment of the optimised asset move plan: the value of '*unmet 4 hours SLA after optimisation*' is 0. The local warehouse RENNES was storing one extra spare compared to the minimum volume needed, which was moved to warehouse PARIS. The other spares were provisioned by the main parts centre (not visible in the table).

Figure 3.6 shows the overall report after optimisation. In the local warehouse PARIS, the asset move optimisation led to a full coverage of service assurance (*MinStock*) for WS-F6700-CFC, X2-10GB-LR, and attempted to reduce the risk for other products CLA-7600 and CISCO7604 but could not fulfil the SLA-wise *MinStock* objective. In this case, the machine recommends investing in or re-evaluating the risk rule.

Analysing the impact for all the products installed and on spare in stock, the overall results show that, before optimisation, the status was:

1. Volume of uncovered MinStock level: 201 spares assets were missing or misplaced.

After optimisation, the status on a real-world use case became:

1. Reduction by 43% of the penalty cost.
2. Volume of uncovered MinStock level: 121 spares required and still missing, so 60% reduction in the volume of misplaced items.

A map view as shown in Figure 3.7, displaying stock nodes (warehouses) and customer sites, allows the visualisation of nodes that have stock and are at risk for a specific asset. It can also be used to rapidly assess the positive impact of the asset optimisation process. In total, 106 contracts of 4-hour SLAs are present and spread over 102 sites. This node is considered at risk with a deficit of 10 items to reach an appropriate level of coverage for those contracts.

The impact of the generated asset moves plan is evaluated as a reduction of the cost potential caused by lack of spare parts and consequently maintenance service failure. This reduction of cost can be derived from the outcome of asset move optimisation planning when the heuristic is guided by the risk rate associated to each asset product. This needs to be balanced against the cost of transferring assets (shipping, packaging) – to avoid moving too frequently and to facilitate a grouped transfer of assets.

Conclusion

Optimising the deployment of assets and the replenishment of spares is key to the successful performance of service organisations. Central to this viewpoint is the ability to model scenarios in dynamic environments. Changes in operations tend to impact the way organisational resources such as assets and spares are utilised to deliver services – a combinatorial and optimisation problem. AI techniques are known for their efficiency in finding good solutions in polynomial time using heuristic search methods and their modelling capabilities to express constraints declaratively. In this chapter, we have presented AI-based approaches for asset management in a service chain. We have described two use cases along the two dimensions of maintaining organisational resources – strategic and operational. We proposed a decision-making approach where AI-constraint propagation and heuristics search techniques are used to proactively recommend the levers for optimising the overall service assurance level and the performance of inventory-dependent services. This enables asset and spare managers to optimise the deployment of mobile warehouses and the replenishment of spares with the objectives of:

1. automating strategic coverage of inventory sites and operational asset decision allocation to warehouses while minimising CAPEX investments;
2. having a list of potential locations for new warehouses and identifying which places are the best located for them, according to a demand profile;
3. recommending warehouse topology changes (removing, resizing) without damaging the asset maintenance service assurance of the organisation;
4. optimising CAPEX while reducing penalties and maximising revenue;
5. optimising minimum and maximum stocks per site/equipment/customer;
6. assessing whether the existing stock in depots is sufficient to cover a given provisioning and fault demand for a given asset;
7. providing the optimised asset move plan given a policy; and
8. estimating what CAPEX investment is needed to meet demand in the event of no feasible plan being found.

Some of the key lessons learnt during the rollout of the capabilities included engaging end users to validate (1) key requirements, and (2) the outputs of the models. We used an agile approach coupled with rapid prototyping in this regard. This approach enabled us to deploy the capabilities right the first time. The capabilities have led to significant operational benefits and better service outcomes for our operational teams. The feedback from the business was excellent, highlighting the flexibility that AI techniques have to offer in asset management in a service organisation.

References

BT. (2019). BT Group plc annual report 2019. Retrieved from: https://btplc .com/Sharesandperformance/Annualreportandreview/2019summary /assets/documents/BT_annual_report_2019.pdf.

Desport, P., Lardeux, F., Lesaint, D., Liret, A., Di Cairano-Gilfedder, C. & Owusu, G. (2016). Model and combinatorial optimization methods for tactical planning in closed-loop supply chains. ICTAI-IEEE 2016 Conference.

Desport, P., Lardeux, F., Lesaint, D., Di Cairano-Gilfedder, C., Liret, A. & Owusu, G. (2017). A combinatorial optimisation approach for closed-loop supply chain inventory planning with deterministic demand. *European Journal of Industrial Engineering, 11*(3), 303–327.

Desport, P., Lardeux, F., Lesaint, D., Di Cairano-Gilfedder, C., Liret, A. & Owusu, G. (2019). A sequence-based metaheuristic for tactical distribution planning in closed-loop supply chains. 9th IFAC Conference on Manufacturing Modeling, Management and Control (MIM 2019), 28–29 August 2019, Berlin, Germany.

Goldberg, D. (1989). *Genetic algorithms in search, optimization, and machine learning.* Addison-Wesley, Boston, MA.

Hooker, J. N. (2012). *Integrated methods for optimization,* 2nd edition. Springer, New York and London.

Larrañaga, P. & Lozano, J. A. (2002). *Estimation of distribution algorithms: A new tool for evolutionary computation.* Kluwer Academic Publishers, Boston, MA.

Liret, A. (2008). Work allocation and scheduling. In C. Voudouris, D. Lesaint and G. Owusu (eds), *Service chain management: Technology innovation for the service business,* (pp. 139–152). Springer, Berlin, Heidelberg.

Owusu, G., O'Brien, P., McCall, J. & Doherty, N. F. (2013). *Transforming field and service operations.* Springer, Berlin, Heidelberg.

Owusu, G. & O'Brien, P. (2013). Transforming field and service operations with automation. In G. Owusu, P. O'Brien, J. McCall & N. Doherty (eds), *Transforming field and service operations with automation: Methodologies for successful technology-driven business transformation,* (pp. 15–28). Springer-Verlag, Berlin, Heidelberg.

Pintov, U. & Brandeleer, G. (2019). IoT and the future of field service. Field Technologies Online, April 2019.

Shakya, S. & Santana, R. (2012). *Markov networks in evolutionary computation.* Springer, Berlin, Heidelberg.

Shakya, S., Kassem, S., Mohamed, A., Hagras, H. & Owusu, G. (2013). Enhancing field service operations via fuzzy automation of tactical supply plan. In *Transforming field and service operations,* (pp. 101–114). Springer, Berlin, Heidelberg.

Shakya, S., Lee, B. S., Di Cairano-Gilfedder, C. & Owusu, G. (2017). Spares parts optimization for legacy telecom networks using a permutation-based evolutionary algorithm. 2017 IEEE Congress on Evolutionary Computation (CEC), 1742–1748.

Taleizadeh, A. A., Niaki, S. & Aryanezhad, M. (2010). Optimising multi-product multi-chance-constraint inventory control system with stochastic period lengths and total discount under fuzzy purchasing price and holding costs. *International Journal of Systems Science, 41*(10), 1187–1200.

Voudouris, C. (2008). Defining and understanding service chain management. In C. Voudouris, D. Lesaint and G. Owusu (eds), *Service chain management: Technology innovation for the service business,* (pp. 1–17). Springer, Berlin, Heidelberg.

CHAPTER 4

Digital Supply Chain Procurement Transformation

Frank Omare

Introduction

Globalisation and outsourcing have created cost efficiencies over the years, as organisations change their operating models to meet global consumer demand. Supply chains are becoming more complex as multiple tiers of suppliers are relied upon to provide the materials necessary to complete and ship finished goods to eager consumers. This complexity creates increased risk and constant pressure to monitor every aspect of the extended supply chain ecosystem. Organisations must be vigilant regarding their extended supply chain to safeguard their own reputations and brands against any damage. News of unethical business practices spreads quickly in the age of the 24/7 news cycle and ever-present social media. These resources allow consumers to be better informed about the products and services they purchase. Consumers are also showing both an increasing desire to purchase products that align with their sense of global responsibility and a willingness to spend more money to do so (Curtin 2018). Producers must be able to prove their viability in such a market or risk failure. In response to these market drivers, organisations must find a way to maintain a clearer view of who they are doing business with.

How to cite this book chapter:
Omare, F. 2022. Digital Supply Chain Procurement Transformation. In: Wang, Y., and Pettit, S. (eds.) *Digital Supply Chain Transformation: Emerging Technologies for Sustainable Growth*. Pp. 61–79. Cardiff: Cardiff University Press. DOI: https://doi.org /10.18573/book8.d. Licence: CC-BY-NC-ND 4.0

Digitalisation has a key role to play to increase visibility and transparency across the supply chain and improve collaboration between business partners to create more purpose-driven supply chains. For many organisations, digital transformation has become a strategic imperative. It improves the connectivity between business partners and increases the access and distribution of critical data. However, many organisations succumb to the potential pitfalls of a digital transformation implementation such as failure to re-engineer their business processes, insufficient resources to deploy the technology and absence of a robust business case. This chapter demystifies digitalisation and illustrates the benefits it brings to the supply chain. Research conducted by strategic consultancies provides insights on the primary focus and outcomes of digitalisation and guidance about how to get started and avoid digital failures.

Digital Revolution

Supply chain models are experiencing a digital revolution that is being driven by the consumer-driven digital economy. Digitalisation will be a fundamental topic for organisations across all industry sectors in the years to come. Data analysed in real time supports collaboration across the supply chain and improves the visibility of inventory. This provides opportunities to optimise sales and operations planning (S&OP) so that inventory levels of raw materials and components can be reduced across manufacturing sites and supplier locations. In turn, this reduces stock picking and loading, handling, stock transfer notifications etc. Therefore, optimised S&OP and inventory levels improves logistics efficiency and reduces operating costs. Also, the working capital tied up in inventory is cut and this drives a positive impact on the balance sheet. Organisations measure such inventory reductions through movement in the days in inventory outstanding (DIO).

Today, there is growing international trade and digital commerce. An efficient supply chain can thrive amid changing priorities by helping control costs, meeting the needs of customers and providing scale. This contributes to an organisation's competitiveness and helps reduce the cost of serving its operations. Better and more efficient supply chains support sustainability and ethical practices in the following ways:

1. supporting people and local communities through responsible sourcing (considers the impact to society and the environment);
2. avoiding risk of workplace and human rights violations in areas such as inclusion and diversity, forced labour, and wage discrimination through improved visibility across the supply chain;
3. reducing waste and spoilage with lean manufacturing;
4. improving crop yield through precision farming with big data, supercomputing and hyperconnectivity;

5. improving resource utilisation and reducing inventory with fully integrated planning and manufacturing;
6. reducing the number of stock and transport movements through better warehouse management, which in turn reduces storage and any associated temperature control requirements for stock; and
7. driving greater levels of efficiency to create more visibility, leading to lower inventory and storage footprint, thereby cutting waste levels and reducing energy consumption (for example, warehousing machinery and vehicle movements, heating, lighting and temperature control).

Procurement needs to take an active role in shaping the digital journey, both within the organisation and at the interface with key suppliers. This strengthens the role of the procurement function as a valued business partner.

In the past, technology-enabled change was mainly aimed at replacing manual processes and making them faster and more efficient, for example through e-procurement and e-invoicing. The push was to reduce cost and increase efficiency. This is ongoing. However, as we move into the digital era, technologies like predictive analytics, robotic process automation (RPA) and artificial intelligence (AI) are also creating entirely new ways of doing things.

The pace of this innovation is relentless in our consumer-driven digital economy. Companies are going beyond the stage of awareness when it comes to digital technologies. They already understand the power of AI, the internet of things (IoT), cloud computing, robotics and mobile applications. Other technologies, such as blockchain, are now appearing on the radar. The digital revolution has several significant business implications, although digital technologies vary greatly in their impact and technological maturity. Organisations need to consider the conditions and layout of their IT architecture strategy to realise the benefits across the procurement value chain.

The six digital accelerators identified by the Hackett Group outline the key requirements for improving a company's procurement performance and supporting its business strategy in the long term (The Hackett Group 2018):

Accelerator #1: Digital Engagement

World-class organisations are service-oriented and customer-centric in their approach to procurement delivery. They actively measure the results of their efforts through formal service level agreements for internal customers.

Accelerator #2: Robotic Process Automation (RPA)

RPA has made a quick entry onto the agenda of procurement and purchase-to-pay organisations to perform routine activities without human intervention.

In procurement, 38% of companies are currently in the piloting stage, indicating rapid adoption. Assuming that the widespread adoption of RPA continues, many procurement organisations believe it will become one of the areas with the greatest impact on the way their work gets done in the period up to 2030, including, for example, touchless processing for the entire purchase-to-pay operations.

Accelerator #3: Analytics-Driven Insight

The hallmarks of information-centric, world-class procurement organisations are the presence of a sophisticated information/data architecture that makes effective data analysis possible; planning and analysis capability that is dynamic and information-driven; and performance measurement that is aligned with the business.

Accelerator #4: Modern Digital Architecture

Results from recent research on the benefits of various software tools are encouraging. In the case of supplier discovery software, the top benefit found was a reduction of up to 31% in the time it takes to find and qualify a new supplier. The research also documented the benefits of e-sourcing software, including the ability to reduce overall cycle time by 30% by using standard templates to reduce data-collection errors. The reported benefits of contract life cycle management (CLM) software include reducing the amount of time required to find a contract by 52%, trimming the number of lapsed contracts by 39%, and increasing the use of standard terms and conditions to ensure compliance.

Accelerator #5: Digital Workforce Enablement

Procurement can leverage modes of communication that appeal to a new generation of workers to create a culture of collaboration and speed up work processes. For example, many world-class organisations have launched social media initiatives and other web-centric spaces to facilitate broad communication.

Accelerator #6: Cognitive Computing

Cognitive computing and artificial intelligence (which seek to mimic the way the human brain works) are in their nascent stages but are starting to help some procurement organisations run models, make predictions and analyse large data sets. For example, a consumer goods company has been relying on a cognitive tool used by a third party to gather data from social networks world-wide to make predictions about potential trouble spots.

Getting started on a digital procurement transformation begins with a business case, as part of 'success planning'. This identifies value, return on investment and payback:

1. There must be a programme vision for the transformation and a procurement strategy that is aligned with the overall business strategy.
2. Spend and transaction data, ideally for a period of 12 months, is analysed. Benchmarks and taxonomy are applied to profile the spend.
3. There should be engagement with stakeholders to understand challenges, business problems and expectations. Interviews and workshops are conducted with targeted subject matter experts and stakeholders.
4. Savings are estimated based on insights from experiences of other transformation programmes and from industry benchmarks. These savings are reported as 'value levers' and include price reduction, compliance, process efficiency and working capital improvement. The total investment is estimated from the cost of the technology and its implementation. From the estimated benefits and investment, the return on investment (ROI) and payback are determined.
5. The business case should be validated with senior stakeholders in the organisation. Change management and training are important considerations for a successful programme and these costs/efforts must be factored in as the business case is finalised and validated.
6. A realistic road map for the implementation should be developed based on the organisational capabilities and technology footprint. This road map will include a 'wave plan' to both onboard and e-enable suppliers. Governance and project management are key to ensuring that the programme delivers the expected outcomes.

Figure 4.1 highlights the SAP 'success planning' model.

Future Role of Procurement

If chief procurement officers (CPOs) are interested in transforming the role of procurement, then digitalisation can provide opportunities to contribute to the wider commercial activities of the organisation. Mergers and acquisitions (M&A) is a powerful example. The current strong M&A market can be expected to continue and the current deal environment can be expected to improve, or at least remain stable. Getting a seat at the table with the C-Suite during M&A activities helps to transform procurement into a strategic role that goes beyond finding and acting on low-hanging fruit opportunities.

Figure 4.1: SAP success planning model.

Pre-Merger

Traditionally, procurement is not involved in the due diligence activities and in the scoping of the potential cost savings from the merger of the two businesses. Typically, an arbitrary savings target of 5% is proposed by consultants and signed off by finance. Given that procurement spend can be up 65% of sales revenues depending on the sector, there are significant opportunities for the CPO to become involved in the strategic planning of a business (*SAP Digitalist Magazine* 2019).

At the pre-merger stage of the M&A, digitalisation can automate and streamline the process of estimating the procurement savings, which is often thought to be too time-consuming. The use of digital solutions allows procurement to extract data from both internal and external sources, cleanse them, and categorise them in enough detail to provide a 'true north' base line position of the combined external spend. Procurement can use the data to identify areas of opportunity and to inform the board of the savings from synergies. This can be done within weeks rather than months.

Post-Merger

After the deal closures, procurement can gain more access to data at the spend category level across the different plants, business units, countries etc.

Next-generation data management captures real-time value from different data sources. Procurement can identify pricing or specification discrepancies between different plants or divisions, spend or supplier fragmentation, and disconnects between raw-material prices and commodity-market indices. This will validate the savings estimate pre-merger or identify gaps where additional savings are required. Organisations are more likely to achieve a thoughtful stretch target based on savings identified using analytics and spend intelligence.

If digital solutions are not available, the M&A activity can present opportunities to develop a business case to invest in a digital transformation post-merger that will help to realise significant savings from cost reduction, compliance, process efficiency and working capital improvement. The procurement team can perform the data analysis and apply taxonomy to profile the spend. They can work with subject matter experts during the discovery sessions to validate spend classification mapping. Benchmarks can then be applied to estimate the savings and the ROI from the investment required in software, implementation and training.

Procurement can offer the M&A an alternative option for cost savings. Accurate data and insights increase the level of confidence in the realisation of the benefits from sourcing activities. Robustly calculated procurement cost savings can reduce the emphasis on need for plant closures and lay-offs of workers. A better way to cut costs is through procurement rather than headcount reduction. Procurement cost savings can deliver an immediate benefit to the bottom line. Headcount reductions, while immediate, take a while for the benefits to be realised owing to redundancy costs and the hidden costs of restructuring programmes. Also, there are missed opportunities to redeploy staff from the duplicated roles and functions, and to strengthen parts of the new organisation. Digitalisation not only provides opportunities to raise the profile of the CPO; it can also provide a more ethical means of delivering savings from M&A synergies that are declared to the stock market.

Building Responsible and Resilient Supply Chains

The Global Financial Crisis of 2007–2008 is considered by many economists to be the worst financial crisis since the Great Depression of the 1930s. The financial crisis was caused primarily by the deregulation of the financial industry and, as a result, many financial institutions collapsed. Supply chains were not immune. Suppliers were unable to borrow money and organisations sought ways to manage their working capital by extending supplier payment terms. These factors compounded to increase the risk of the financial collapse of suppliers. During this period, risk management was observed to be typically ineffective. The consequences of supplier failure could be significant across several areas, as illustrated in Figure 4.2 below.

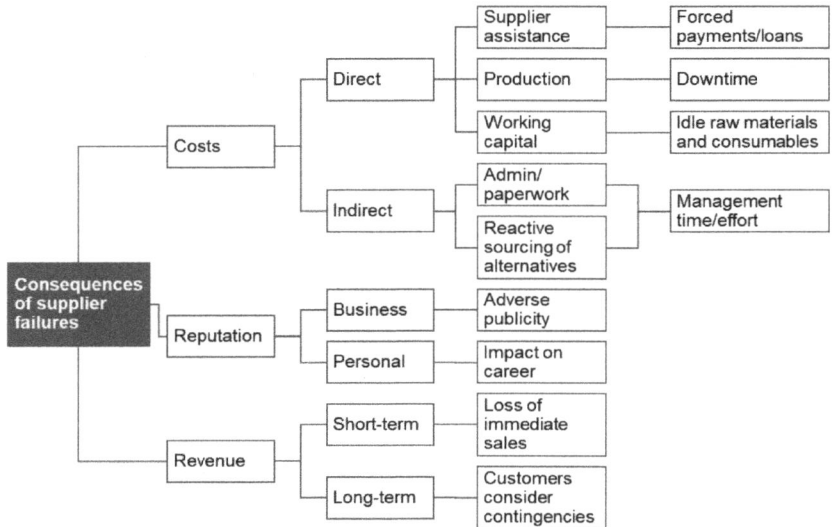

Figure 4.2: The consequences of supplier failure. Source: EY (2011).

CPOs realised that good procurement balances the need for cost savings with the health of key suppliers. Traditional indicators to predict the risk of supplier failure could not be relied upon. It became clear that smaller 'strategic' suppliers can have significant impact on business performance if they fail suppliers who provide goods and services of relatively low value and quantity can stop big brands being produced and sold globally. The risk management lessons from the last economic downturn in 2008 are applicable to building responsible and resilient supply chains today. There is a need for proactive risk management that uses digital technology to process data from multiple sources to identify risk exposure to social and environmental issues. Today, supply chains typically include multiple partners, with services and sourcing managed across many organisations and around the world (Figure 4.3).

Recent surveys conducted by the Category and Sourcing Managers Executive (CASME) have indicated that the top challenges facing procurement include risk management, reputation and brand image and corporate social responsibility (CSR) (Chartered Institute of Purchasing & Supply Chain 2017). Brands with purpose are proven to outperform those without purpose by a factor of three (BrandZ 2017). There is clearly more pressure for brands to behave more ethically than before. Yet, procurement is typically still focused on sourcing and continues to be measured on year-on-year costs savings.

The CPO needs to fully understand the organisation's sustainability goals and determine how procurement connects with these operationally. The CPO has a very influential role to play here with supplier risk assessments, sourcing, contracts, supplier performance management and compliance with procurement policies and codes of conduct. Negotiated payment terms should protect the

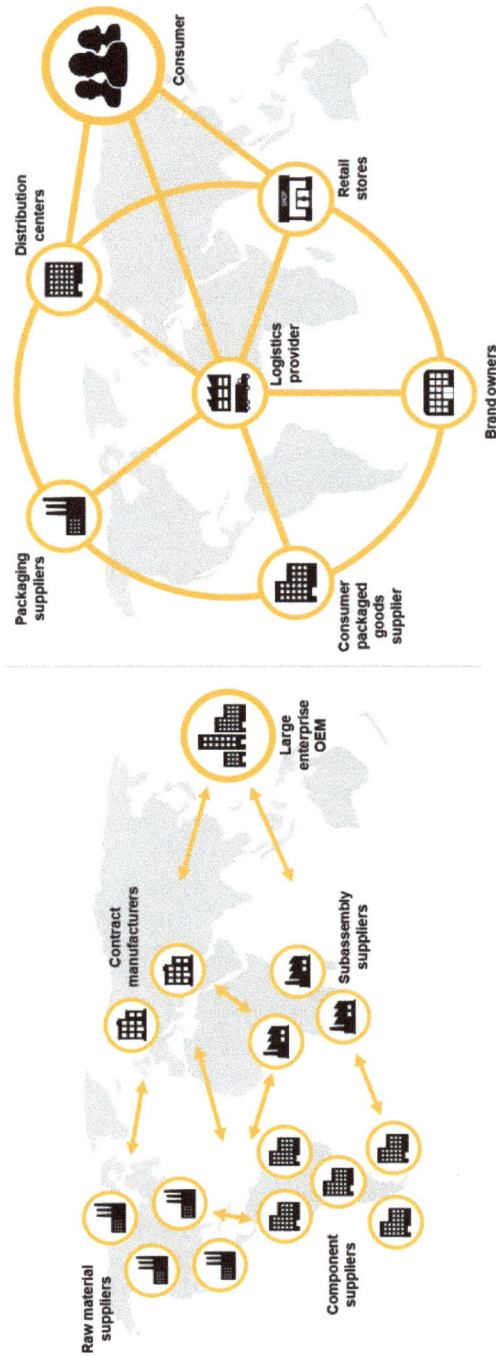

Figure 4.3: Complexity in today's supply chain. Source: Omare (2017a).

working capital of suppliers so that workers are paid promptly, particularly in industry sectors or countries where there is a high risk of slavery.

The UK's Buy Social Corporate Challenge is a groundbreaking initiative that sees leading corporates open their supply chains to include social enterprise suppliers, which are typically small or medium-sized businesses committed to having a social impact, such as the employment of disabled people and protecting wildlife ecosystems. Organisations thereby become a means of support for local communities, creating opportunities and employment where few had existed before. Through being part of this initiative, companies can both diversify and drive innovation in their supply chains, using their procurement function to change how they buy goods and services. SAP issued a press release about a partnership with Social Enterprises UK, the national body in the UK.

LONDON, United Kingdom — April 17, 2019 — SAP (UK) Limited plans to strengthen its support of the social enterprise sector by making it even easier for organisations to find and do business with certified social enterprises on Ariba® Network, the digital marketplace where more than £2 trillion in business-to-business commerce is conducted annually. As the official technology partner of Social Enterprise UK, the expert body for the UK's social enterprise sector, SAP aims to facilitate better connections between corporate buyers and other employees with social enterprises, helping them spend better and in a more socially and environmentally sustainable way (Sap News, 2019).

Technology not only helps to connect social enterprises with corporate organisations but can also tackle known challenges in bringing scale and efficiency to the creation of ethical supply chains. For many organisations, initiating a programme for purpose-driven procurement can be daunting. Often there are insufficient resources available to conduct the due diligence necessary to determine suppliers' sustainability and fair labour practices. Supplier risk solutions provide ongoing and scalable risk intelligence that can help organisations detect early warning signals, minimise costly disruptions and proactively monitor risk factors for each supplier. With these solutions, organisations can identify and assess the sustainability risks for new suppliers and monitor those for current suppliers.

Further, finding a diverse range of suppliers can be a challenge for buyers. Unlocking opportunities with large organisations can be equally difficult for small minority-owned suppliers. Digital supplier networks can help buyers discover and connect with diverse suppliers, opening the door to new relationships and business opportunities. These opportunities can also be extended to social enterprises.

However, data mining and mapping provides valuable insights into the activities and processes operated across the supply chain. Action can also be taken to remove inefficiencies and unnecessary steps to create win–win scenarios for supply chain partners. The removal of cost inefficiencies can fund the investment in payments to primary workers in the supply chain. Also, intelligent technologies such as blockchain can support the cost breakdown analysis across the value chain from 'farm to fork', 'bean to cup' and so on, to verify that primary workers receive a fair wage in relation to the total cost of the product. The streamlining and automating processes create the bandwidth for procurement to explore more opportunities to do good in addition to delivering the cost savings agenda.

There is also an opportunity for organisations to use their influence to improve the human, economic and environmental impact of every organisation that their supply chain touches. This is often defined as 'procurement with purpose'. Over the years, procurement with purpose has made its way into boardrooms of large and small organisations alike – across all industries and geographies. Purpose is considered to be useful in driving business growth and employee productivity and loyalty. It also helps establish an organisation's status as an employer of choice and preferred business to business (B2B) purchasing partner. This is an important factor when broader issues such as environmental concerns are receiving much greater levels of attention. It has been suggested that 'By 2025 three quarters of the world's working population will be millennial. They define companies by what they are doing to make a difference, from speaking out on social issues to placing environmental justice at the core of what they do' (Paul Afshar, head of purposeful business at FHF, quoted in Sacre 2018). In this context, 'purpose' has a much greater role to play.

There has never been more pressure on brands to operate ethically. Due in large part to the rise in social media, public opinion about a brand can now go viral in an instant. Consumers are increasingly aware of negative impacts on the environment and question where and how products are made. More and more consumers are choosing purpose-centred brands that promote transparency in their supply chain, use sustainable sources of raw materials, and employ fair human and environmental practices. Purpose is no longer something that is nice to have; it has become a strategic imperative that is high on every organisation's agenda if it wants to be perceived as relevant, admired and innovative by its customers, employees, investors, partners and communities. There are many quoted examples of supplier risk management failings in complex, extended supply chains:

Human Rights Watch (HRW) reported 25 May 2016 the use of child labor in tobacco plantations in Indonesia, whose harvest supplies local and foreign tobacco companies. Children, some of whom are just eight years old, are exposed to nicotine, handle toxic chemicals or use dangerous tools in extreme heat (*San Diego Union Tribune* 2017).

Children as young as 14 have been employed to make clothes for some of the most popular names on the UK high street, according to a new report. Workers told investigators that they were paid as little as 13p an hour producing clothes for UK retailers (*The Guardian* 2017).

Organisations are responding to these needs with the creation of sustainable supply chains. The question 'what if this could be achieved?' therefore arises, as Figure 4.4 shows.

Traditional business models aim to create value for shareholders. This is often at the expense of other stakeholders. Purpose-led businesses are redefining the

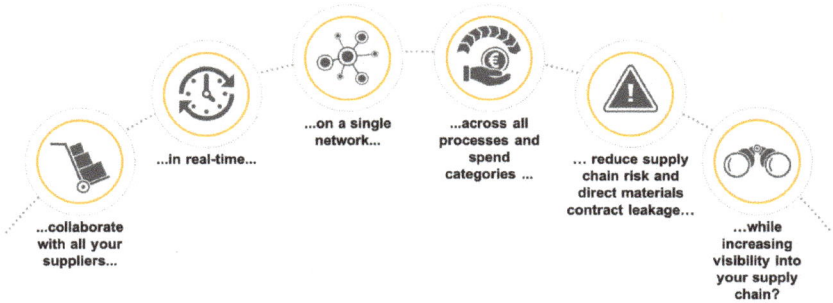

Figure 4.4: Supply chain collaboration. Source: Omare (2017b).

value chain by designing models that create value for all stakeholders, supply chains, communities and the planet. Complex supply chains bring inherent risk. They extend around the world and are vulnerable to the influence of poor labour conditions, natural disasters and conflict. They also face the issue of increased resistance to globalisation, as local supply chains are now perceived as more ethical from an environmental perspective. Despite these challenges, there are opportunities for organisations to help improve the human, economic and environmental impact on every society and organisation they touch. Globalisation has resulted in the rise of global partners through global supply chains as organisations seek to leverage scale and synergies in sourcing and supply chain operations. However, globalisation has placed many local and small to medium-sized organisations (SMEs) at a disadvantage. In response to this, many organisations have developed sustainability initiatives that are designed to help SMEs in the local communities in which they operate.

Responding to Climate Change

Around the globe, governments are confronting the reality that, as human-caused climate change warms the plant, rising sea levels, stronger storms, increased flooding, harsher droughts and dwindling freshwater supplies could drive large populations from their homes. The poorest and most vulnerable are most likely to suffer the impacts of climate change (Schwartz 2018). This demonstrates a direct correlation between global warming and the social and economic sustainability of people who reside in countries vulnerable to climate impacts.

The landmark Paris Agreement in 2015 between the parties to the United Nations Framework Convention on Climate Change (UNFCCC 2019) was a major step towards combatting the effects of climate change on a global scale. This concern about climate change extends beyond the UN and federal government level to all areas of both the public and private sector. Those aligned with the goals of the agreement have vowed to take steps to establish and adhere to practices that actively reduce their contribution to global warming. The key elements of the agreement are detailed in Table 4.1.

Table 4.1: Key elements of the Paris Agreement 2015.

Keeping the global temperature increase 'well below' 2.0°C (3.6°F) above pre-industrial levels, with the goal of reducing that amount further to 1.5°C.
Limiting the amount of greenhouse gases emitted by human activity to the same levels that the trees, soil and oceans can absorb naturally, beginning at some point between 2050 and 2100.
Requiring all members to establish and communicate a nationally determined contribution (NDC) with reviews every five years to assess each country's progress and set new goals.
Encouraging developed countries to help developing nations by providing 'climate finance' – funds to help adapt to climate change and switch to renewable energy.

Source: UNFCCC (2019).

Many companies have committed to becoming carbon neutral within a specified time frame to help reduce global warming. A review of the sustainability reports of several global companies provides insight to the actions being taken to respond to climate change in their supply chains. For example, Unilever aims to reduce its environmental footprint by 50% by 2030 (Unilever 2019), Carlsberg is committed to zero carbon footprint by 2030 (Carlsberg Group 2017), GlaxoSmithKline (GSK) has set a target to be carbon neutral by 2050 (GlaxoSmithKline 2019) and Shell has set targets for 2035 and 2050 (20% reduction in carbon footprint by 2035 and 50% reduction by 2050) (E&T 2018).

Other ways organisations can commit to running their businesses in a more sustainable manner include:

1. setting up business forums and networks to encourage suppliers to share best practices on sustainability;
2. implementing packaging redesigns that reduce environmental footprint;
3. supporting developing countries to strengthen their scientific and technological capacity to move towards more sustainable patterns of consumption and production;
4. protecting natural resources through energy waste and water management and preserving biodiversity;
5. measuring energy efficiency and using low-carbon energy sources;
6. reducing emissions;
7. reclaiming more waste for beneficial reuse, recycling and recovery and striving to add zero waste to landfill;
8. increasing the share of renewable energies in the total energy mix;
9. creating a low-carbon advantage and developing the organisation in support of the Paris Agreement and United Nations Sustainable Development Goals ambitions.

Relationship Between Business Behaviours and Brand Value

There is now more value placed on brand identity, customer loyalty and employee engagement. Business behaviours impact the balance sheet's intangible assets such as goodwill, customer lists and intellectual property. Figure 4.5 highlights a fivefold increase in the relative value of intangible assets on the balance sheet between the years 1975 and 2015 (Ocean Tomo 2017). Purpose-related behaviours therefore now have a more significant impact on organisations than ever before. Further, Figure 4.5 illustrates the components of S&P 500 market value based on market capitalisations of the 500 largest companies having common stock listed on the NYSE or NASDAQ (S&P 500).

Companies with strong performance in sustainability outperform the market by 4.8% and gain cheaper equity financing owing to reduced risk (Columbia University 2016). Sustainable investments now account for a large proportion of the stock market. Globally, nearly $60 trillion is managed by more than 1,300 investment firms that have signed up to the UN Principles for Responsible Investment. In 2006, there were only 100 signatories, controlling approximately $6.5 trillion (Rotchild 2017).

Procurement is best placed out of all corporate functions to drive the purpose agenda. It is procurement that manages the sourcing activities and contract awards, develops supplier and other third-party relationships and manages compliance with codes of conduct (both internally and externally). In addition, procurement has a role to play in ensuring the organisation sources in an ethical manner that protects our natural resources and rewards suppliers that avoid unfair labour practices. The development of diverse supply chains not only brings innovative ideas and solutions to organisations but it can also help increase competitive advantage and market growth. Transacting with

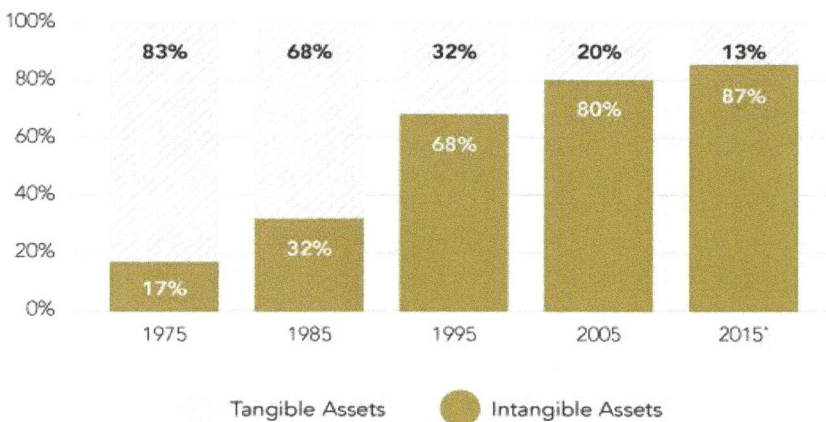

Figure 4.5: Components of S&P 500 market value based on market capitalisation. Source: Ocean Tomo (2017).

small minority-run organisations helps reduce socio-economic inequality and boost local economies.

Procurement can manage provenance effectively across supply chains that are enabled by digitalisation. With blockchain, transaction data is bundled into digital blocks. Each new block is linked to the previous block, creating a continuous chain. When a block gets added, the blockchain node sends the data to the network to be verified by all the other nodes. This triggers a consensus algorithm for authenticity. This ensures that no one can undo the block, remove an old transaction, or create a new block to cover up any wrongdoing. For example, data is available at every part of the supply chain to trace raw materials or components to the point of their origin. Also, companies can use the same technology to track the price build-up for produce across the supply chain and gain visibility of the supply chain partners profit margins in relation to the price paid to farmers.

Procurement has the ability to drive positive impact on society and the environment during each state of a procurement cycle, as shown in Figure 4.6.

There are several non-financial pressures that support the case for investing in a purpose-driven business. Organisations need to realise the importance of how their behaviours are perceived, e.g. respect for the local communities in which they operate and paying the living wage. Further, those with stronger sustainability performance can reduce their average turnover over time by 25–50% and reduce their annual quit rates by 3 to 3.5%. Consumer expectations are also rising, with nearly two thirds of consumers believing they have a responsibility to purchase products that are good for the environment and society. From an organisational perspective, around 60% of investors view non-financial disclosures as essential or important to investment decisions. Finally, stock exchanges and governments are increasingly issuing requirements for companies to report on corporate responsibility data in annual reports (Whelan & Fink 2016).

For any organisation, leading with purpose means a number of actions have to be taken. These include: training suppliers to recognise the warning signs of modern slavery and consider the environmental impact of their operations; aligning procurement practices with human rights due diligence (for example, lead times, prices and support given to implement code of conduct requirements); and supporting social enterprises through initiatives such as Buy Social Corporate Challenge in the UK. Further there is a need for the monitoring of environmental risks to minimise impact on the well-being of people and the planet, and investing in technology to improve collaboration with supply chain partners and increase transparency and responsiveness.

Modern supply chains can include multiple partners, with services and sourcing managed across many organisations and around the world. Supply chains are becoming more complex across extended ecosystems. This reduces visibility into supply and drives up supply chain risks, including the use of forced labour. There is clearly more pressure for brands to behave more ethically than

1 Identifying vulnerability and risk (prioritizing products)

2 Understanding prioritizing and dealing with risk (in supply chains)

3 Supplier market engagement and development of procurement plan

4 Evaluation and shortlisting of suppliers (including pre-qualification followed by creation of invitation to tender or request for quotation information packs)

5 Evaluation of quotes or offers and preferred supplier selection

6 Creation of contract and performance management against contract

7 Update ethical procurement program (share and reward good practice)

*Source: Chartered Institute of Procurement & Supply (Modern Day Slavery Act 2015)

Stages 1 and 7
Stages 1 and 7 focus on the ethical/responsible purchasing program, covering all purchases

Stages 2–6
Stages 2–6 are the stages a purchasing organization goes through in relation to each purchase

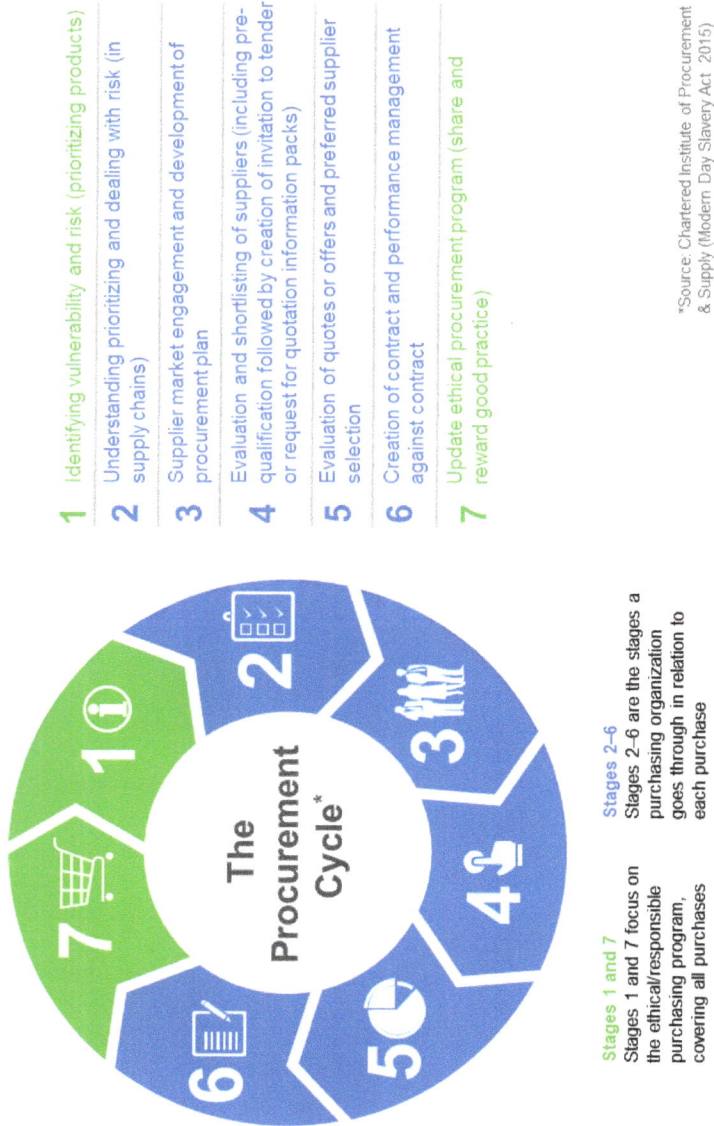

Figure 4.6: The procurement cycle. Source: Chartered Institute of Purchasing & Supply (2015a).

before. Yet, procurement is typically still focused on sourcing and continues to be measured on year-on-year costs savings. How can we tackle this complex dilemma? Is procurement prepared, or even authorised, to pay more for products sourced ethically? Is procurement prepared to terminate and invoke harsh penalties for bad practice or even develop their own suppliers?

As mentioned previously, the CPO needs to fully understand the sustainability goals of the organisation and determine how procurement connects with these operationally. The Buy Social Corporate Challenge is a groundbreaking initiative that sees leading corporates open their supply chains to include social enterprise suppliers. For example, SAP has integrated into its supply chain Brewgooder, a craft beer social enterprise that donates 100% of its profits to clean water projects around the world. Thus, without compromising on quality, SAP's purchases are directly providing clean water access, with a stated target of reaching more than 1 million people by 2025 (Brewgooder 2019).

Without question, more consumers are choosing brands based on sustainable sources and raw materials and on fair human and environmental practices. 'Purpose' is no longer something that's nice to have; it's become a must-have strategic imperative that is high on every organisation's agenda if they want to be perceived by their customers, employees, investors, partners, communities, and public entities as relevant, admired and innovative. Procurement has a role to play in driving forward the purpose agenda.

Society is demanding that companies, both public and private, serve a social purpose. To prosper over time, every company must not only deliver financial performance, but also show how it makes a positive contribution to society. (Larry Fink, CEO, BlackRock, in the *2018 annual letter to CEOs* (BlackRock 2018)).

Conclusion

Digitalisation is helping organisations to transform their procurement operating models to stay ahead of the challenges of today's complex supply chain. Organisations are redefining their business models, operating processes and work. This trend is set to continue as technologies emerge as part of the digital revolution. Organisations need to consider the key requirements for successful deployment of digital technologies. Effective risk management been a challenge since the last global economic downturn. We experienced the collapse of supply chains due to the inability to suppliers to finance their work capital requirements. Today, digital technologies enable organisations to analyse data for multiple sources and convert into intelligent insights. This, coupled with real-time processing, allows organisations to identify risks and mitigate them. These risks include social and environmental issues that impact brand value and image. Digitalisation can provide opportunities for the CPO to contribute to the wider commercial activities of the organisation.

References

BlackRock. (2018). BlackRock Larry Fink's 2018 chairman's letter to shareholders. Retrieved from: https://www.blackrock.com/hk/en/insights/larry-fink -ceo-letter [accessed 28 April 2019].

BrandZ. (2017). Top 100 most valuable global brands 2017. Retrieved from: https://brandz.com/report/global/2017 [accessed 18 April 2019].

Brewgooder. (2019). The craft beer on a mission. Retrieved from: https://www .brewgooder.com [accessed 29 November 2019].

Carlsberg Group. (2017). Carlsberg to achieve zero carbon emissions at its breweries by 2030 as part of industry-leading sustainability ambitions. Retrieved from: https://carlsberggroup.com/newsroom/carlsberg-to-achieve-zero -carbon-emissions-at-its-breweries-by-2030-as-part-of-industry-leading -sustainability-ambitions [accessed 28 April 2019].

Chartered Institute of Purchasing & Supply. (2015a). The procurement cycle, Modern Slavery Act 2015. Retrieved from: https://www.cips.org/Docu ments/Knowledge/Procurement-Topics-and-Skills/4-Sustainability-CSR -Ethics/Sustainable-and-Ethical-Procurement/3/Modern-Day-Slavery.pdf [accessed 28 April 2019].

Chartered Institute of Purchasing & Supply. (2017). Top six challenges facing procurement. Retrieved from: https://www.cips.org/en-sg/supply-manazge ment/opinion/2017/september/the-top-six-challenges-facing-procurement- [accessed 18 April 2019].

Columbia University School of International and Public Affairs. (2016). Quantifying the costs, benefits and risks of due diligence for responsible business conduct. Retrieved from: https://mneguidelines.oecd.org/Quantifying -the-Cost-Benefits-Risks-of-Due-Diligence-for-RBC.pdf [accessed 18 April 2019].

Curtin, M. (2018). 73 percent of millennials are willing to spend more money on this 1 type of product. Inc. https://www.inc.com/melanie-curtin/73 -percent-of-millennials-are-willing-to-spend-more-money-on-this-1 -type-of-product.html [accessed 18 April 2019].

E&T. (2018). Shell pledges to reduce carbon emissions by 50 per cent by 2050. Retrieved from: https://eandt.theiet.org/content/articles/2018/12/shell -pledges-to-reduce-carbon-emissions-by-50-per-cent-by-2050 [accessed 28 April 2019].

EY. (2011). Consequences of supplier failure P.15. Retrieved from: https://www. cips.org/Documents/Membership/Branch%20Event%20uploads/1025154 _Supplier%20risk%20management_CIPS%20Presentation_May%202011 .pdf [accessed 28 April 2019].

GlaxoSmithKline. (2019). Our commitments. Retrieved from: https://uk.gsk .com/en-gb/responsibility/our-planet/our-commitments [accessed 28 April 2019].

The Guardian. (2017, 5 February). How high street clothes were made by children in Myanmar for 13p an hour. Retrieved from: https://www.the

guardian.com/world/2017/feb/05/child-labour-myanmar-high-street
-brands [accessed 28 April 2019].

The Hackett Group. (2018). Raising the world-class bar in procurement through digital transformation. Retrieved from: https://www.thehackettgroup.com /wp-content/uploads/2018/06/hackett-world-class-pro-1806.pdf [accessed 18 April 2019].

Ocean Tomo. (2017). Intangible market asset value study. Retrieved from: https:// www.oceantomo.com/intangible-asset-market-value-study [accessed 18 April 2019].

Omare, F. (2017a). *SAP Ariba complexity in today's supply chain*. Internal report. Unpublished.

Omare, F. (2017b). *SAP Ariba supply chain collaboration*. Internal report. Unpublished.

Rotchild, L. (2017). Does corporate social responsibility influence our stock price? Huffington Post. Retrieved from: https://www.huffingtonpost.ca/leor -rotchild/does-corporate-social-responsibility-influence-our-stock-price _a_23015651 [accessed 18 April 2019].

Sacre, R. (2018). Is CSR slowly dying? FleischmanHillard Fishburn. Retrieved from: https://fhflondon.co.uk/2018/07/is-csr-slowly-dying [accessed 18 April 2019].

San Diego Union Tribune. (2016, 25 May). HRW reports use of child labor in Indonesian tobacco production. Retrieved from: http://www.sandiegounion tribune.com/hoy-san-diego/sdhoy-hrw-reports-use-of-child-labor -in-indonesian-2016may25-story.html [accessed 28 April 2019].

SAP Digitalist Magazine. (2019, 23 April). How procurement can create value in mergers and acquisitions. Retrieved from: https://www.digitalistmag.com /finance/2019/04/23/how-procurement-can-create-value-in-mergers -acquisitions-06197885 [accessed 28 April 2019].

SAP News. (2019). SAP Backs Social Enterprises Through £2 Trillion Pro-curement Platform. Retrieved from https://news.sap.com/uk/2019/04/sap -backs-social-enterprises-through-2-trillion-procurement-platform/ [accessed 10 October 2019].

Schwartz, E. (2018). Quick facts: How climate change affects people living in poverty. Mercy Corps. Retrieved from: https://www.mercycorps.org/articles /climate-change-affects-poverty [accessed 18 April 2019].

Unilever. (2019). Sustainable living. Retrieved from: https://www.unilever.com /sustainable-living [accessed 28 April 2019].

United Nations Framework (UNFCCC). (2019). What is the Paris Agreement? Retrieved from: https://unfccc.int/process-and-meetings/the-paris-agreement /what-is-the-paris-agreement [accessed 18 April 2019].

Whelan, T. & Fink, C. (2016). The comprehensive business case for sustainability. *Harvard Business Review*. Retrieved from: https://hbr.org/2016/10/the -comprehensive-business-case-for-sustainability [accessed 18 April 2019].

CHAPTER 5

An Introduction to Flexible, On-Demand Warehousing: E-Space

Andy Lahy, Katy Huckle, Jon Sleeman and Mike Wilson

Introduction

A highly flexible, agile supply chain has become a key requirement for many businesses to remain competitive (Kumar, Shankar & Yadav 2008). In today's multi-channel, fast-paced and highly demanding marketplace, both manufacturers and retailers must be able to produce and deliver products faster than ever before. It is no longer just about minimising supply chain costs. Increasingly, the speed of supply chain is the key differentiator when it comes to making a sale or losing out to the competition.

With most of the world's products manufactured in a different country, or even on a different continent, to the one where they are eventually sold, guaranteeing a quick delivery is no mean feat. And if, as expected, trade barriers and tariffs continue to develop, then delivering across borders will only become more difficult in the future (King 2018).

The only way for companies to achieve the short lead times demanded by today's consumers is to store products in large, centrally located warehouses.

How to cite this book chapter:
Lahy, A., Huckle, K., Sleeman, J., and Wilson, M. 2022. An Introduction to Flexible, On-Demand Warehousing: E-Space. In: Wang, Y., and Pettit, S. (eds.) *Digital Supply Chain Transformation: Emerging Technologies for Sustainable Growth*. Pp. 81–98. Cardiff: Cardiff University Press. DOI: https://doi.org/10.18573/book8.e. Licence: CC-BY-NC-ND 4.0

This is how most supply chains currently work: products are manufactured on one side of the world, they are then shipped to a central warehouse for storage, where they sit and wait, until finally they are delivered to the end customer.

Although this supply chain model has served many companies well for the last 20 years, the rapid acceleration of consumer expectation for immediate delivery (largely driven by increasing online purchasing) has drastically outpaced the speed at which supply chains have adapted. In short, customer demand for speed has increased tenfold, whereas the speed delivered by global supply chains has yet to change.

The most common way companies have sought to meet this consumer demand for faster deliveries is not by completely changing the supply chain but rather by adding more inventory in more warehouses. The result is an explosion of inventory across supply chains, with billions of products sitting idle in warehouses, costing money and losing value.

The effect of this increase in inventories can be seen in the rapid increase in the number of warehouses built: in the USA alone there is over 9.1 billion square feet of warehousing space (the equivalent of more than 200,000 football pitches), with over 1 billion square feet of warehousing added in in the last 10 years alone (CBRE 2018). However, the cost of these warehouses pales into significance when one considers the value of the products stored inside them – estimates put this figure at over $1.2 trillion (Federal Reserve 2018).

With such a high value of inventory held in supply chains, why haven't they adapted to keep up with the increasing demand for fast delivery? One reason is that the contract logistics market is anything but adaptable. Logistics service providers (LSPs) cling stubbornly to outdated business models; they are stuck and slow to innovate (Cui, Shong-Lee & Hertz 2009). Furthermore, LSPs demand long-term warehousing contracts, volume commitments and accurate forecasts to lock their customers into fixed supply chains. As one supply chain manager explained, 'warehousing remains the last fixed element in the supply chain'.

In this chapter, we will discuss the reasons why the existing contract logistics model is not suitable for the fast-moving, adaptive supply chains of today. The chapter begins with a brief introduction to how the contract logistics industry currently works, before introducing a new model, hereafter referred to as E-Space, which we believe will turn the existing contract logistics model upside down. In doing so, E-Space will free up manufacturers and retails to implement the flexible, fast and agile supply chains that we as consumers demand.

Our vision for this new world does not stop there. It is not just contract logistics that is holding back the transition to more flexible supply chains; manufacturing also remains stubbornly slow to adapt to the new world. We conclude the chapter by proposing that once the slow, fixed nature of the contract logistics model is disrupted, that of manufacturing will not be far behind.

The Warehousing Industry Today

The commercial need to transport products from point of origin to point of consumption has existed as long as there have been products (Wilkinson et al. 2009). However, the rapid rate of globalisation over the last 30 years has meant that supply chains have become elongated and complex. Most shippers (organisations that produce or sell products) have elected to outsource their logistics operations to LSPs, rather than invest in their own planes, boats, trucks or warehouses. The idea of providing warehousing as a service started to develop as an industry in the late 1980s (Sheffi 1990). Since then, the warehousing industry as a whole has experienced tremendous growth, exemplified by the establishment of multinational LSPs such as DHL, UPS and FedEx. Today, the outsourced warehousing industry, commonly referred to as the contract logistics industry, is worth over $200 billon (BCG 2016).

The logistics industry really took off when the world went global and demand for outsourced logistics surged. Manufacturing moved to low-labour-cost countries; the rise in consumerism created more demand in more markets; international transportation grew at double-digit annual growth rates; and technological advances meant that products could be managed across continents. But setting up a new warehouse is not as simple as it may first seem. As described in Figure 5.1, it usually involves nine steps and takes from six to nine months. A timeline of more than two years is not uncommon if the warehouse must be built from scratch.

The first step is in the supply chain design, which involves identifying the need for a new warehouse (or multiple warehouses) to improve the supply chain. The next step is to select the size and location for the warehouse(s). Warehouse location selection usually begins with a centre of gravity study. This study is a mathematical modelling of the best possible location for a warehouse based on product supply and demand. The calculation for the location of a facility or facilities will determine the coordinates of the best location(s). A typical example of the outputs from a centre of gravity study where either one or two locations are desired is shown in Figure 5.2.

Typically, once a shipper can estimate the new warehouse location and approximate size, they will send out a request for information (RFI) to find existing options in that market. This allows LSPs to respond with their availability and options. This process can be problematic, as if the volumes are very large then LSPs will struggle to provide enough space. If volumes are too small, LSPs may choose not to respond at all to the RFI, as the potential returns are not worth the required time investment to sign a contract.

In most cases, a number of potential suppliers are identified, allowing the shipper to create a request for quotation (RFQ), which is essentially a request for the exact cost of implementing and operating that warehouse. The RFQ process in itself can be very slow, as shippers need to define their exact

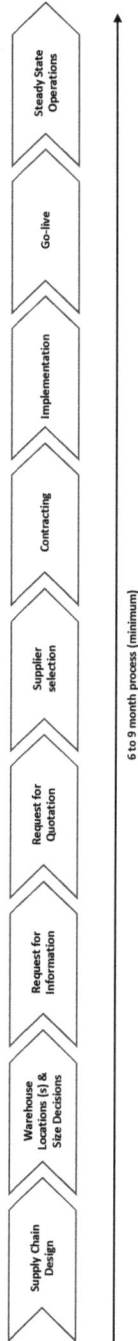

Figure 5.1: Steps needed to set up a new warehouse.

Centre of gravity analysis of customer network with one central location	Centre of gravity analysis of customer networks with two central locations

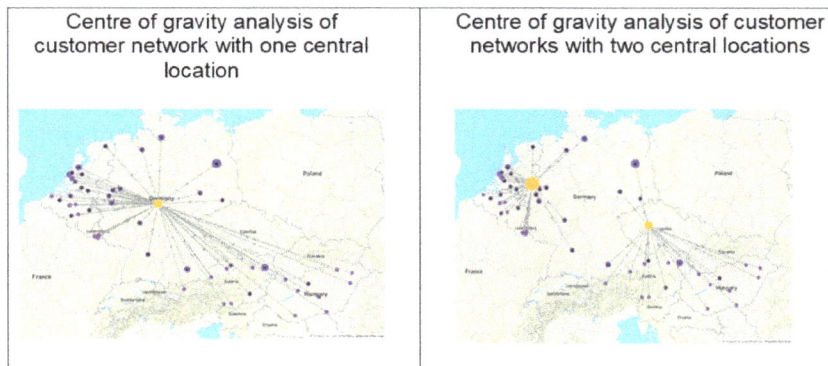

Figure 5.2: Centre of gravity analysis to select number and location of warehouses.

business requirements (volumes, number of orders, order profiles, types of products to be stored, any specific system requirements). Both short-term and long-term requirements must be mapped. This information is essential for the LSP to provide a quote.

It is at the RFQ stage that the process becomes difficult, and therefore slows down. Shippers are asked to predict their volumes and order profiling over the next three to five years, which most would agree is an impossible task. But LSPs will not commit to renting and operating a new warehouse without guaranteed volumes and revenue; they refuse to accept any exposure or risk. Predicting the future space and labour requirements of any business is a guessing game, and often the LSP relies on a long list of assumptions to calculate their quotation. With each LSP applying different assumptions and calculation methods to calculate their pricing, the next step in Figure 5.1, the supplier selection step, can prove notoriously difficult.

As soon as the pricing model has been agreed, a quote provided, and the customer is ready to sign on the dotted line, then surely it should be smooth sailing from there on in? Sadly not. It is not uncommon for contracts between LSPs and customers to run into hundreds of pages, as the nuances of scope of services, liabilities and service levels are carefully defined. The contract seeks to cover as many possible variations in business outcome as possible; it is usually a case of: if you can imagine it happening, then it needs to go in the contract.

Finally, though, all the contracting is complete, everything is signed, and the implementation phase can begin. Typically, implementation takes between eight and 12 weeks to complete. While there are occasional exceptions, and some implementations are possible in a week, the majority take longer, especially if new hardware must be ordered, staff trained, or new warehouse management systems (WMSs) established and integrated with existing systems.

When we sum up all of these timelines (up to three months for the pricing, another month or more for contracting, and up to three months for implementation), it is not at all surprising that customers complain about the glacial speed of LSPs. The time between the shippers' decision to establish a new logistics operation and the first customer order leaving the warehouse frequently exceeds six months. In these six months, both parties are focused solely on the basics of the contract; there is no mention of innovation or process improvement, let alone how the LSP can help its customers achieve their strategic objectives. The bureaucratic contracting process leaves little time for anything else.

It is only after implementation that both the shipper and LSP can really see if the original assumptions (used for all the pricing and contracting phase) were correct. Unsurprisingly, the assumptions often turn out to be incorrect, and so the negotiations continue throughout the life of the contract; the bureaucracy of adjusting prices and contracts continues until the shipper has the energy for a change.

A New Approach: E-Space

How can flexibility, agility and innovation be introduced into the warehousing industry? To answer this question, we only need to look to the other major sources of disruption in the global business environment. Digitalisation seems to be the key when it comes to improving speed and efficiency. This applies equally to shopping (Amazon), taxi cars (Uber) and tourism (Airbnb). Airbnb works by allowing property owners (suppliers) to advertise their free space to people visiting that area (customers). Space is then booked and paid for through the platform. This process is fast, efficient and low risk.

So why not apply an Airbnb-type solution to warehousing? The result would be an E-Space model that would allow manufacturers and retailers (shippers) to rent short-term warehousing space from building owners and landlords (suppliers) in the same way that holidaymakers rent space in people's homes (Wilson & Huckle 2018). If suppliers could advertise available space via an E-Space platform, and customers could see and then book that space in real time, then the amount of unused space in the overall warehousing network would reduce, and customers could quickly find and book flexible space.

Initially, this seems like a simple solution, but selling warehousing is not quite as simple as creating an online market place and sitting back as the business floods in. Digitalising a long, complex process will not automatically make things faster. Thereby, in order for an E-Space model to work for warehousing, the process itself must be readdressed. A digital warehousing marketplace would provide visibility on where to find empty space, but, if LSPs cannot simplify their pricing in order to sell that space, the utility of any E-Space platform would be extremely limited. Pricing for basic warehousing space must therefore be immediately available, along with an indication of handling costs, so that potential customers can calculate and compare possible options.

Table 5.1: Requirements of an E-Space model.

Pricing	Immediate pricing available on the platform for the space. Indicative pricing for handling costs must also be provided.
Contracting	A simple contracting process that allows customers, suppliers and LSPs to quickly agree on prices and contracting terms.
System	A fast, online warehouse management system that can be operational in hours, not weeks or months.
Transportation	Integrated transport rates and systems, which allow customers to book and pay for not just the warehouse but also all activities up to and including the customer delivery and any returns.

A further challenge that remains, even with a warehousing marketplace, is the duration of implementation. Even if customers are able to find warehousing space, and contract with the owner quickly, the process of setting up a new warehouse still would take weeks or even months. Implementing a warehouse management system and integrating with customer ordering systems is a slow process. To truly act as a flexible system, E-Space needs to improve the speed of implementation. The E-Space business model must also address the challenge of transportation to and from the warehouse. Customers will need total visibility on transport cost and availability before directing inventory to new warehouses, and they need that information before they can even select a new warehouse location. Without this visibility, the trade-offs between one warehouse location and another will remain unknown.

Moreover, customers now expect full traceability on their products throughout the supply chain. The most sensible approach here would be to integrate transportation with the E-Space business model; this saves customers having to contract with a multitude of different transport providers in numerous different warehouse locations. In summary, the E-Space business model needs to provide more than a simple market place between warehousing customers and suppliers; it must remodel the existing warehousing process into something agile, fast and flexible. The key stages of this process are detailed in Table 5.1.

Implications of E-Space for Supply Chains

What would happen to supply chains if companies could use an E-Space platform to store inventory close to customer demand in any available warehouse, instead of the warehouse selected three years previously? Look again at the centre of gravity analysis provided in Figure 5.2. What if, rather than trying to find one central location and committing to a three-year contract, manufacturers and retailers could make use of multiple warehouses, store goods in warehouse A today and warehouse B tomorrow, without any long-term contracting, and

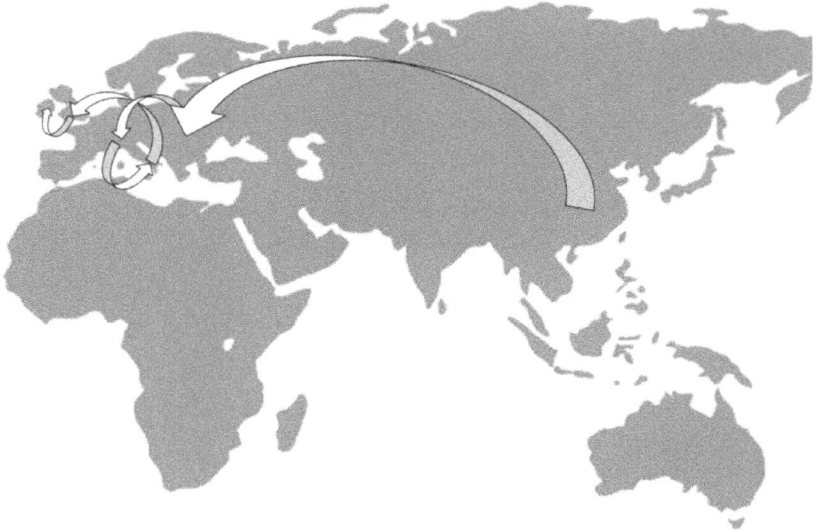

Figure 5.3: A complex, nonsensical transport flow in a supply chain from China to Ireland.

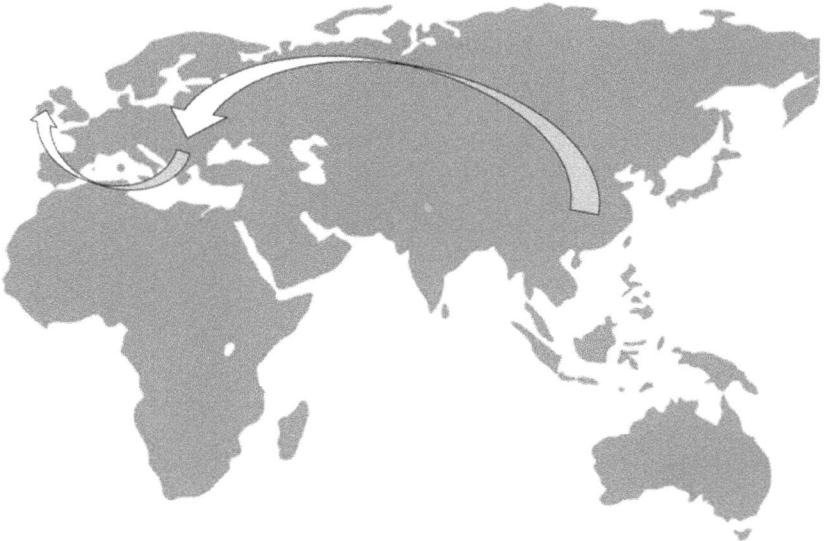

Figure 5.4: An E-Space-facilitated supply chain with transport from China to Ireland through central Europe.

depending on product flow and customer locations? What would be the impact on the logistics world? What would E-Space mean for supply chains in general, as well as inventory levels and final-mile transportation?

The possibilities introduced by the E-Space model could turn global supply chains upside down, in particular the contract logistics industry. Instead of a slow, over-contracted and change-resistant industry, logistics could become a fast-paced, agile and flexible environment. Customers would be able to make decisions on warehousing in real time, and we would see far greater movement of products from locations with lower demand to those with higher demand.

When it comes to inventory management, the impact of E-Space could be enormous. The current lock-in system of today, where warehousing customers sign long-term contracts for space, makes it almost inevitable that the warehouse will become full of inventory. Warehouses are a bit like suitcases or spare rooms: the bigger they are, the more you find to fill them. And, of course, if you are already paying for warehouse space because you are locked into a fixed-term contract, it would seem like an overall cost advantage to manufacture in bulk and store excess products in a warehouse. This seems to make sense, but take it further and it means that companies over-produce (because they have space), store too many products, and then leave them there indefinitely. LSPs regularly stock products for years, even decades, because their customer refuses to bite the bullet and scrap unwanted goods, even if it is clear to all involved that those goods will never be sold.

The fixed nature of contract logistics also has negative implications on transport cost. Because warehouses are fixed points in the supply chain, transportation of goods must be organised around them. This often results in nonsensical transport flows (Figure 5.3), where products move from the port or airport of entry to a centrally located warehouse, before moving back along the same road to deliver to customers who live next to that port or airport.

If organisations could store products across small warehouses close to local demand, rather than large, central warehouses in the middle of nowhere, then transport effort and cost could be greatly reduced (Figure 5.4). This would lead to a clear benefit for supply chains in general but also the wider environment and the many road networks struggling under traffic congestion.

Implications of the E-Space Model for Users

Even when the technology is there, an industry that has worked one way for 20 years is not going to change overnight. But change it will. In this section we provide insight from three different stakeholders that will be affected by the transition from contract logistics to E-Space:

1. **Suppliers** (landlords and real estate)
The implications of an E-Space model for suppliers are major. Through an E-Space platform, they will gain access to vast network of customers who will

specifically be looking for warehousing space. Suppliers will be able to sell empty space for short periods of time, charging a premium for flexibility and last-minute contracting. The warehousing market will open up into a free market, where price will be derived purely from market demand. Suppliers will easily be able to hedge risk by operating for a larger number of smaller customers instead of depending on one or two large customers.

2. Customers (shippers)

The warehousing market as it is today leads to massive amounts of waste in the supply chain. This waste can be product waste (many products disappear into rigid, elongated supply chains) or space waste. Below is a typical example of how customers currently end up with unwanted warehousing space:

What the customer needs:	What the LSP offers:	What the customer gets:
10,000 square metres, January–November 15,000 square metres, December	A fixed contract of 15,000 square metres January–December	A monthly invoice for 5,000 unused square metres for 11 months of the year

An entire supply chain cannot be changed overnight, but the E-Space approach has massive implications for customers. If customers decide to use an E-Space platform, it may be for either strategic or tactical supply chain decision, as well as a combination of both. Strategically, customers could redesign their entire warehousing and delivery strategies to be as flexible as possible while still maintaining quality standards. For example, matching product warehousing to customer demand in real time would ensure that products are always correctly placed to supply customers, without any excess space and the associated costs. Tactically, customers could solve problems such as peak season excess inventory by temporarily employing the E-Space model to seek out additional space at critical times.

What the customer needs:	What E-Space offers:	What the customer gets:
10,000 square metres, January–November 15,000 square metres, December	Flexible space throughout the year to match demand on a month-by-month basis	No unused warehousing space, locations that match up with demand, and the ability to make changes when needed

Additional implications for customers include access to a vast network of suppliers, reduced commitment to long-term contracts and much less pressure to predict their future demand.

3. **Warehouse operators** (LSPs)

Regardless of what happens in the E-Space sphere, there will always be a need for vast warehouses in the middle of the desert to store toilet paper, toothpaste and the student staple dried noodles with a 70-year shelf-life, so the contract logistics model is not going to disappear completely. But, for perishable products, or those that become obsolete very quickly (e.g. fast-changing technologies), then a simple E-Space model could well replace the traditional LSP when it comes to sourcing warehousing space.

The LSP must then find other ways to add value in the supply chain. This will often involve warehouse management, as this is something that the majority of suppliers prefer to outsource. LSPs also need to find ways to add value to the products themselves, for example through packaging, labelling or even more advanced manufacturing services such as assembly or testing.

4. **Consumer** (end customer)

There are also implications of the E-Space model for the end customer, who will find their products arriving more quickly than ever before. The carbon footprint of products purchased online may reduce as their journeys become more direct, so there is an argument for increasing sustainability of supply chains. Prices will also be impacted as product manufacturers and retailers no longer need to pay for excess inventory, a cost that is inevitably passed to the end customer.

Industry Perspective: On-Demand Warehousing (JLL)

Warehouses are critical components in virtually all supply chains. However, while the latter are increasingly being challenged to be more agile and responsive to changes in customer demand, warehouses are fixed assets which offer their users only limited flexibility at best. They are fixed in terms of location and often have limited potential to flex capacity.

Users (businesses and other organisations) that have a need for additional warehouse capacity have traditionally had three options: to own or lease an additional facility and operate it themselves; to own or lease a facility and outsource the operation to an LSP; or to outsource the facility and operation to an LSP on either a dedicated or a shared/multi-user basis. Whichever option is chosen, sourcing an appropriate solution often takes months and involves a long-term commitment (such as a lease or a contract with an LSP) typically measured in years, although short-term contracts are available for shared/multi-user contracts. These timescales are fundamentally at odds with the ability to respond quickly to changes in customer demand or to service customers in ever-shorter time frames, which the growth of e-commerce especially has highlighted.

Given these dynamics, it is unsurprising that the markets for both warehouse real estate and warehouse/logistics services are being disrupted by technology platform providers, such as Stockbooking in France and FLEXE in the US, that seek to connect users of warehouse space with providers of warehousing and services. These platforms enable users to source warehousing and services on-demand from a large network of approved suppliers on a 'pay as you go' basis without long-term commitments – a model that JLL refers to as 'warehouse as a service' (WaaS). These providers could be LSPs or other non-LSP occupiers who have spare capacity within their warehouses.

These types of platforms have existed for years in the road freight industry, enabling cargo owners to source transport capacity as and when required, via online 'freight exchanges', but they are relatively new in the market for warehouse real estate and warehouse/logistics services. While all these platforms digitally connect users with suppliers, different network providers offer different services. For example, in France, Stockbooking says that: 'Storage spaces and logistics services offered will depend exclusively on the offer of the selected partner.' In the US, the FLEXE offer includes access to the FLEXE technology platform, a cloud-based WMS that warehouse providers use to manage FLEXE projects, and which users utilise to manage and track inventory, orders and shipments. The FLEXE offer also provides users with access to a team of dedicated logistics coordinators to manage their day-to-day needs across their network of FLEXE facilities.

Although the on-demand market is fully digitised by the different platform providers, it is not, in aggregate, transparent. As a result, it is not possible to provide an indication of the scale of user demand satisfied by on-demand warehouse solutions in the same way that it is possible to scale the demand for traditional warehouse solutions by quantifying how much warehouse space has been transacted via the traditional options of owning, leasing or outsourcing. Therefore, at present, the significance of on-demand warehousing in terms of its impact on the overall demand for warehouse space cannot be assessed. This is not likely to change any time soon unless all the different platform providers report statistics on their business volumes in terms of warehouse space (or capacity) transacted.

Although it is not possible to measure this market, we think there are good reasons to believe it will grow in the years to come. For warehouse users requiring additional capacity, the model offers access to a huge market of suppliers and the opportunity to add (or subtract) additional warehouse capacity when and where required. Some users may choose to use on-demand warehousing and services to supplement a core network of facilities that they own, lease or outsource on a long-term basis, while others could potentially move to a wholly on-demand solution. For those supplying capacity, it offers access to a huge market of end users and the opportunity to secure additional revenues through utilising spare capacity. In addition, for landlords (as opposed to warehouse suppliers that are also occupiers) the on-demand model may provide an alternative way to market a property, especially if that property is having difficulty attracting interest from users on a traditional long-term basis.

Clearly, the on-demand solution will not suit all warehouse users, in the same way that a traditional outsourced solution does not suit all businesses. Very many businesses will continue to want to have their own long-term facilities, especially where they also make large investments in automation and robots. In addition, without a stock of warehouses occupied on a long-term basis by LSPs or others it would not be possible for the technology platform providers to offer the on-demand service to others.

If, as we expect, on-demand warehousing expands as a way of sourcing both warehouse real estate and warehouse/logistics services, this will clearly be disruptive for the existing markets. Real estate brokers who traditionally market warehouse properties on behalf of users or landlords or act for users in sourcing appropriate buildings (or sites) are likely to adapt with their own digital marketplaces to provide more flexible solutions, and LSPs who traditionally offer dedicated or shared user services are likely to add on-demand services to their offering by creating digital platforms that embrace their existing warehouse stock.

The logic of the on-demand model is that users can provide more efficient and responsive logistics services to customers from a stock of warehouse buildings that are more fully utilised than would otherwise be the case. If this proves to be the case, then on-demand warehousing could make supply chains more sustainable as well as more flexible. This potential win–win outcome means that everyone with an interest in real estate or logistics should follow developments in-demand warehousing closely.

Limitations of the E-Space Model

The biggest challenge facing the E-Space model will be convincing the customer market to accept a modal shift in how they acquire warehousing space. While the current process is lengthy and inefficient, this is what customers are used to. If another option offers the same service in only a fraction of the time, suspicion will naturally arise that the service is inferior in some way, and therefore not to be trusted. Market confidence comes from experience – we trust what we know. This is the major challenge for any new business model that dramatically changes how markets operate. We know the success stories – Uber, Airbnb, Expedia, to name but a few – but for every success story there are many thousands of failures where the market did not accept a proposed change.

For warehousing customers, using an E-Space platform requires placing trust in a network of unknown suppliers. While a warehouse provider may offer the right amount of space in the right location at the right price, if the provider is an unknown company or even a private individual, then warehousing customers will be wary about signing a contract with this provider. And rightly so – if you need to store products essential for the continuation of your business, then you want to be certain that the person responsible for them is to be trusted. Insurance policies or legal battles are no use when your entire product line has been lost or destroyed through careless handling; your end customers will simply find a new supplier and your business is perhaps irreparably damaged.

How to control quality of service is therefore another major challenge for the E-Space model; if an E-Space platform offers a network of warehousing suppliers, it must offer some method of quality control. Established, long-running and trustworthy suppliers must be able to demonstrate their competence in some way that the customer can easily understand. New suppliers must also be able to compete in the warehousing market space in order to promote fair competition. Photographs are the simplest way for a customer to see exactly what they are buying; video links are even better, as are 360-degree tours of a building.

E-Space platforms could also offer supplier certification systems: visiting and auditing warehousing suppliers to ensure service provision is up to standard. Generally, the more detail that a warehousing supplier can provide about the space, the more confidence the customer will feel placing their products there. A user rating system is also a common way for previous customers to share their experiences, which over time builds a picture of the level of service on offer. As warehousing is highly KPI-driven, ongoing monitoring and evaluation is relatively easy to envisage, whereby warehouse providers could share their service KPIs (without revealing customer details) and therefore provide a clear overview of their warehousing capabilities.

Another potential challenge to the E-Space model is product liability: what happens when things go wrong? Storing large volumes of valuable goods in one place inevitably leads to the risk of something becoming lost or damaged. In the regular warehousing model, there is one customer (the owner of products) and one supplier (the owner of space). It can be that the supplier has been outsourced by an LSP, but in that instance the LSP is the supplier, at least as far as the customer is concerned. In an E-Space model there is an additional supplier in play: the platform provider. This increases the complexity of the customer/supplier relationship and leads to additional questions about relationship ownership and also liability.

If the platform provider is purely a middleman linking the customer with the warehousing supplier, with no guarantee of quality, no relationship with either party, and no investment in the success or failure of the warehousing transaction, then it is very easy for the platform provider to accept no liability whatsoever for anything that happens in the warehouse. If, however, the platform provider does want to guarantee quality or to retain customers, then it has an obligation to ensure that standards are maintained and to provide assistance if they are not. This leads to a complex question about the extent of liability E-Space platform providers should be willing or able to accept, and this question is an issue for the entire model.

The final challenge we address in this chapter is that, should platform providers simply act as a middleman linking customer with warehousing supplier, what is to stop those parties from bypassing its system in any and all future transactions? If the platform merely introduces two parties and enables them to do business together, taking a small cut of that business, then should those parties decide to do business in future they will communicate directly and cut out the middleman. The platform must add value to the business transaction either through guarantees of quality, risk mitigation, more competitive pricing or some other method. How to add value is a challenge already faced by many existing E-Space providers.

Taking the Flexible Approach Even Further

What are the further implications of an E-Space approach to supply chains? If manufacturers and retailers can quickly and easily decide where to place products, with guaranteed transportation links and final delivery assurances, then this will open up a huge range of opportunities to move value up and down the supply chain, to decentralise non-critical processes, and to take advantage of the local market that your end customers call home. In this final section we explore just a few of the possibilities opened up by the E-Space model of supply chain.

Pop-Up Factories

No doubt most of us are now familiar with the 'pop-up' concept, where businesses open in a new location for a very limited period of time in order to showcase their products and services or to serve a particular market (e.g. festivals, holidays). We frequently see pop-up restaurants and pop-up stores. What we do not often see are pop-up factories, although Nokia's 'factory in a box' is a step in that direction. E-Space could change that. If manufacturers can use an E-Space model to find the right location to store goods, what is to stop them from using the model to find the right location to produce them? If flexible space is all they need, and E-Space provides that, then why shouldn't manufacturers source production space via an E-Space model? Manufacturing processes can easily be located either directly where the raw materials are available or where the end customer needs the product. Pop-up factories would provide ideal temporary locations for one-off production or short-term contracts. Manufacturers could bring their own machines and employees, needing only the space and the transportation links to run their businesses from anywhere in the world.

Distributed Manufacturing

A natural next step from pop-up manufacturing locations is a strategy of decentralised or distributed manufacturing (Wilson 2017). E-Space is a major enabler of this kind of strategy, as it encourages the idea of relocating products and services close to the end user. The main benefits of distributed manufacturing include reduced lead times, minimal costs of storage, easier customisation and personalisation, and reduced waste. Final products are stored in the component stage, assembled to order and then shipped.

Obviously, the benefits of centralised manufacturing are lost with this approach: economies of scale and cheap labour become less available, at least in the final stages of production. Quality control becomes harder with a distributed model, although today's production controlling technologies facilitate a much easier monitoring of decentralised processes. Pricing, regulations, staff training and many other factors are also more complicated with a distributed manufacturing approach, but these are all solvable and are arguably outweighed by the benefits of such an approach.

Local Sourcing

Linked to the model of distributed manufacturing is the option of local sourcing. If manufacturing can go local, so can procurement, and E-Space could further enable manufacturers to switch to local procurement strategies to reduce their overall environmental footprints. Local sourcing strategies find raw materials in the local, regional or national market where production or fulfilment will take place. For example, if the company Bags Ltd needs to produce in Spain and sells to customers in Spain, then the sourcing strategy with the lowest environmental impact would be to source the raw materials and components for their bags directly in Spain.

There are many challenges associated with local sourcing when it comes to duplicating production and product quality worldwide; obviously, raw materials differ according to where they have been sourced. Managing consistency is critical across different markets if manufacturers want to produce and sell the same products in different markets using locally sourced materials. On the other hand, why do we need everything to always be the same? Would it matter if consumer products in Spain had a slightly different texture or colour to those in Argentina? Arguably, for many products, local variation due to the differences between locally sourced raw materials would be a source of value rather than a problem.

Circular Economy

A final implication of E-Space is that it facilitates a more circular supply chain by making it easier for organisations to recover products (circular economy). Local locations close to the end customer will make it much returns processes much easier for manufacturers and retailers; returned goods can be quickly assessed for faults in the local warehouse, and then either resold back in to the market if no fault is found, or stripped back into components for reuse or recycling. This means that far fewer waste will be generated at the end of product life, which is the main aim of a circular model of supply chain. Valuable products or components are recovered and not lost in to landfill (or worse). E-Space can bring organisations closer to their end customers and help them to maintain better control over the full product life cycle.

Conclusion

Supply chains have a long way to go before they are fully able to satisfy the growing demand for flexibility and agility now coming from the consumer and customer market. Warehousing is still dominated by long-term, fixed contracts. Market players are well established, and everyone knows and understands the system. The industry will not change overnight. However, E-Space is actually already happening. Several flexible warehousing platforms have launched over recent years both in the United States and in Europe. These platforms offer a marketplace of flexible warehousing space through a network of suppliers.

Customer demand for these platforms is still relatively low as awareness of this new business model is still limited. But it is only a matter of time until E-Space platforms become as normal as flight booking, hotels, and transport platforms. As customers start to realise the benefits of updating their warehousing strategies to a flexible, agile model, then we will see a major shift in the market away from the long-term warehousing contracts towards the E-Space model.

E-Space will not work for everyone; if products show very stable demand along with low levels of obsolescence, then it is currently difficult to see the need for flexibility in warehousing. Especially if this flexibility comes at a premium. Mass-produced products with long shelf-lives such as kitchen roll and soap show no current need for agile warehousing strategies – they must simply always be available and volume requirements are easy to predict. But for products with flexible demand, which may be seasonal or related to current trends, or high levels of obsolescence, such as technology, then E-Space is an optimal approach to warehousing strategy. Decisions about where to place products and when are critical to the success of such products. No one will order Christmas trees if they arrive on 26 December. And no one will pay a premium for a mobile phone once the latest model has been released. Delivering product quickly can be make or break for an organisation, and this is highly dependent upon logistics.

There are a number of other challenges facing the new approach: legal and financial questions remain, and, as for the business model itself, how best to approach the establishment of an E-Space platform would need at least another dedicated chapter. The change will not happen overnight, but slowly the modus operandi will shift, which will have major and far-reaching implications for supply chain and production strategies. The inevitable conclusion is that E-Space spells the end of contract logistics as we know it.

References

BCG. (2016). Transportation and logistics in a changing world. Retrieved from: https://www.bcg.com/publications/2016/corporate-development-finance-value-creation-strategy-transportation-and-logistics-in-a-changing-world [accessed 22 April 2019].

CBRE. (2018). Old storage: Warehouse modernization in early stages. Retrieved from: https://www.cbre.us/research-and-reports/US-MarketFlash-Warehouse-Modernization-Early-Stages [accessed 22 May 2019].

Cui, L., Shong-Lee, I. S. & Hertz, S. (2009). How do regional third-party logistics firms innovate? A cross-regional study. *Transportation Journal, 48*, 44.

Federal Reserve. (2018). Federal Reserve economic data.

Flexe. (2019). Warehousing & fulfilment, reinvented. Retrieved from: https://www.flexe.com [accessed 22 May 2019].

King, S. D. (2018). *Grave new world: The end of globalization, the return of history.* Yale University Press, New Haven, CT and London.

Kumar, P., Shankar, R. & Yadav, S. S. (2008). Flexibility in global supply chain: Modeling the enablers. *Journal of Modelling in Management, 3*, 277–297.

Sheffi, Y. (1990). Third party logistics: Present and future prospects. *Journal of Business Logistics, 11*, 27.

Stockbooking. (2019). FAQ. Retrieved from: https://www.stock-booking.com/faq [accessed 22 May 2019].

Wilkinson, A., Dainty, A., Neely, A. & Schmenner, R. W. (2009). Manufacturing, service, and their integration: Some history and theory. *International Journal of Operations & Production Management, 29*, 431–443.

Wilson, M. (2017). *The new world of manufacturing.* PARC Res. Cent.

Wilson, M. & Huckle, K. (2018). *Redefining the contract in contract logistics.* PARC Res. Cent.

CHAPTER 6

Towards a Shared European Logistics Intelligent Information Space

Takis Katsoulas, Ioanna Fergadiotou and Pat O'Sullivan

Background and Business Context

Towards Smart, Green and Integrated Transport and Logistics

Transport and logistics (T&L) is a major component of modern production and distribution systems and is a key contributor to macroeconomic development, accounting for over 10% of gross national product (GNP) in most countries (Savy 2016). The T&L sector is experiencing substantial change (Christopher 2016), influenced by factors such as globalisation, smart specialisation, population growth, business competition, and consumer interest for products from all over the world (Clausen, De Bok & Lu 2016; Leinbach 2007). The sector is also heavily influenced by customer expectations for fast goods delivery, with increased flexibility, at low or close to zero delivery charges. Alongside this, the growth of e-commerce has incited digitalisation in the T&L sector, where, over the past decade, technological advances have been exploited and integrated across the T&L value chain as a whole

---

How to cite this book chapter:
Katsoulas, T., Fergadiotou, I., and O'Sullivan, P. 2022. Towards a Shared European Logistics Intelligent Information Space. In: Wang, Y., and Pettit, S. (eds.) *Digital Supply Chain Transformation: Emerging Technologies for Sustainable Growth.* Pp. 99–119. Cardiff: Cardiff University Press. DOI: https://doi.org/10.18573/book8.f. Licence: CC-BY-NC-ND 4.0

(PWC 2019) to minimise supply chain dwell times and costs. This, in turn, has driven an increasingly competitive landscape where a growing number of supply chain (SC) actors are striving to optimise their SC and/or T&L configurations (Geissbauer et al. 2013; Manners-Bell 2016), often differentiating them according to their customer segment, to achieve more efficient and fine-grained control over their SC performance, as well as better economic, operational and environmental performance.

From a macroeconomic perspective, the European Commission's (EC) strategic vision for Europe also recognises that the T&L sector represents approximately 15% of global GDP annually, with substantial potential for innovation-led initiatives that can incentivise new value imperatives (Savy 2016). Logistics is also one of the most dynamic sectors of the EU economy, contributing to economic growth and international competitiveness. Europe is currently a leader in logistics (World Bank 2014) and, with the steady growth in freight volumes throughout Europe, the long-term forecast is 80% growth in freight transport by 2050 (EC 2015a). With this predicted growth, a pertinent and ongoing challenge is to raise the efficiency and competitiveness of the logistics sector while reducing environmental impacts. Market intelligence confirms that the sustainability of the logistics sector is challenged by its energy consumption and greenhouse gas (GHG) emissions. In order to reduce emissions, logistics actors have started to implement environmentally friendly collaborative strategies addressing supply chain integration, multimodal transport, consolidation of deliveries and reverse logistics (EC 2015b).

However, the sector has several challenging inefficiencies, e.g. a context where only 10% of logistics services are represented by pure transport services and the balance of 90% represented largely by inefficiencies in matching demand and supply of goods and low utilisation of T&L resources (such as empty journeys, idle times, loading and unloading). Consequently, underpinning the EC's strategic vision is the acknowledgement that ICT-driven innovation to date has been hindered by legacy T&L ICT management systems and solutions (thousands) that have evolved incrementally (and oftentimes in bespoke ways) over many years to yield a highly fragmented cross-sectoral logistics ICT landscape across the European SC sector. This challenging context largely resulted in the prevailing T&L ICT solutions that are (today) deeply rooted in legacy technologies and incompatible electronic data interchange (EDI) systems that evolved over many years, and which have not been designed or redesigned in the context of anticipating or supporting collaboration logistics models or cross-sectoral collaboration within or outside Europe. Consequently, today's T&L actors need to contend with multiple tools and solutions covering different aspects of the supply chain, as well as patchy views of their logistics businesses that are difficult, or perhaps impossible, to reconcile and unify into one consolidated business perspective. The implementation of such strategies frequently requires reactive and proactive coordination based on information exchanges between collaborating actors, to optimally match supply and demand for logistic resources. This necessitates real-time monitoring of supply chains, generating vast amounts of data and requiring sophisticated analysis, in order to support tactical and strategic decision-making, creating winning advantages for both businesses and authorities.

In this context, the EC's strategy for Smart, Green and Integrated Transport and Logistics highlighted the need for a common communication and navigation platforms for pan-European logistics. Likewise, a central goal asserted by the Commission was to boost the competitiveness of European T&L industries and to achieve a European transport system that is resource-efficient and environmentally friendly, as well as safe and seamless for the benefit of all citizens, the economy and society. This strategy recognised that advances in the sector have evidenced new international/intermodal repositories and data pipelines being created, management systems being deployed, and new data mining capabilities being developed to deal with the data flood needed for logistics decision-making (European Commission 2015c).

Central to the EC's strategic vision for Europe was steering attention to architectures and open systems for information sharing and valorisation, in pursuit of connecting key stakeholders with information and expertise on the basis of trusted business agreements. More fundamentally, the EC's vision for T&L recognised that the prevailing landscape challenged this strategic view, on the basis that the sector comprised a complex spectrum of different data types and usages that involved disparate and oftentimes legacy information systems that over the years had matured independently and differentially across the EU SC sector's actors, resulting in different user requirements, different business models, different deployment trajectories and incompatible systems that could not share data or intelligence in ICT-driven ways. This broader prevailing digital landscape evidenced an obstacle for inter-sectoral and cross-sectoral information sharing in significant ways, as well as impeding the deployment of pan-European logistics solutions accessible by logically related actors in the transport sector, its users and public authorities.

Thus, the evolving T&L landscape set the scene for creating innovative collaboration-driven supply chain optimisation, supported by services that take into account network status and service level agreements (SLA) for optimising cargo flows against throughput, cost, speed, time, utilisation of resources and environmental KPIs between and across European T&L SC actors. This prevailing context underpinned the innovation imperatives for the SELIS project, which aims to present a solution to these issues.

Industry Requirements

Supply chain actors across Europe and globally (producers, retailers, shippers, logistics service providers, authorities) need a secure a trusted vehicle to share data and information for better horizontal and vertical supply chain collaboration and optimisation. Key business imperatives include the need to surmount the organisational and associated (often internal) structural barriers to collaboration (Figure 6.1), as well as to see progress on a range of operational aspects (Fawcett 2015; McKinsey 2021) including increased speed and efficiency, greater flexibility, improved insights through transparency and granularity, improved prediction and accuracy and improved sustainability.

Principally, SC actors are seeking ways to extract value from shared industry data as well as maintain full control over their own commercially sensitive data, including whom they share data with, the duration of time data is shared, and the ways shared data is used, managed and exploited. Consequently, supply chain actors across Europe and globally (producers, retailers, shippers, logistics service providers, authorities) need a secure and trusted vehicle to share data and information for better horizontal and vertical supply chain collaboration and optimisation. However, although the need for collaboration and data sharing is well understood by the SC and logistics sector, resistance remains high and aligning innovation to industry readiness is very important in moving forward.

The Shared European Logistics Information Space (SELIS) Project

The SELIS project is part of the European Union's Horizon 2020 Research and Innovation Programme and was funded under 'Call MG-6.3-2015' for common communication and navigation platforms for pan-European logistics applications. The project began on 1 September 2016 and was conducted over a

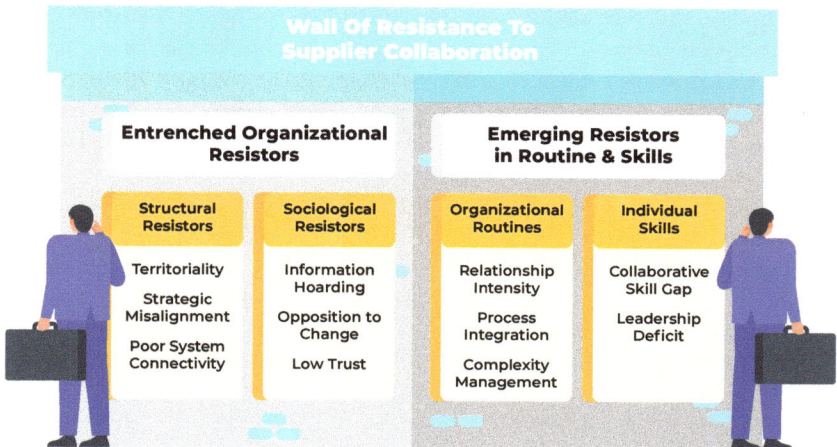

Figure 6.1: Obstacles to better horizontal and vertical supply chain collaboration.

three-year period, finishing on 31 August 2019. The project team comprised 38 separate partners spanning the range of supply chain actors.

Supply Chain Community Nodes (SCNs)

The SCN Premise

The principal innovation from the SELIS project is a directory of logistics collaboration models (LCMs) (Figure 6.2) and connect–share–optimise open-source software components enabling stakeholders in the logistics sector to create and maintain collaborative SC intelligence-sharing platforms, referred to as SELIS community nodes (SCNs). SELIS's approach and contribution towards a 'pan-European logistics intelligence-sharing platform' emphasise intelligence sharing through SCNs in a way that inspires trust, facilitates collaboration and enables connectivity and data-driven optimisation of T&L operations. Extensibility is catered for through a cloud computing platform that accommodates a SC modelling framework for business applications. SCNs can be used to build T&L collaboration solutions that are resource-efficient and environmentally friendly.

Further, federated SCNs provide a solution for the EC's strategy for Smart, Green and Integrated Transport and Logistics through a single European logistics information space that is accessible by actors in the transport sector, its users and public authorities. The SELIS approach is consistent with the Digital Transport and Logistics Forum (DTLF) federated network of platforms

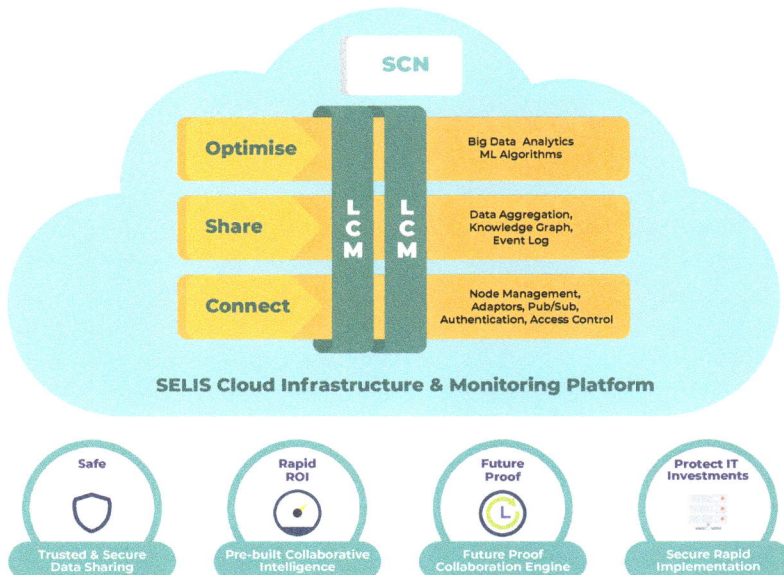

Figure 6.2: The SCN concept.

concept (DTLF 2018) and provides a route towards the realisation of a physical internet (PI)-inspired transport system, aimed at transforming the ways physical objects are packaged, transported, distributed and delivered (Simmer et al. 2017). In essence, from its proposal stage, SELIS has advocated that a promising route to realising the PI vision is through federation of SCNs, a subject that is further discussed later in the chapter.

Features of SELIS Supply Chain Community Nodes (SCNs)

The SCN creates a shared intelligence 'data space' configured to address the needs of a logistics community, aggregating information flows in various industry standard formats that are generated by the operational systems of the logistics participants, and also through interfaces to IoT devices and gateways.

An SCN combines collaboration, connectivity, communication, privacy and data protection capabilities with analytics and visualisation tools, enabling end-to-end visibility across value chains towards the management of business and green logistics KPIs. In SCNs, the connections between the SC participants are managed by rules that describe relationships from the outset and based on their semantic properties such as their role in the SC, rather than on hard-coded connections and data. In this way, an SCN can be considered a multiparty collaboration intelligence-sharing gateway, alleviating the need for costly, isolated and fragmented point to point connections between individual participants in the SC.

In consequence, as the SC evolves (i.e. participants join and leave) the SCN can readapt and reconfigure autonomically to address the evolving and changing circumstances. The result is near-real-time insights and enhanced visibility such that the stakeholders in the logistics value chain can improve their operations, plans, policies and strategies, as well as quality of service aspects central to their business KPIs.

Specifically, an SCN supports T&L communities to (Figure 6.2):

1. Connect: allowing data to be collected from heterogeneous sources, thus creating a single data-sharing intelligence space in the cloud, which physically consists of distributed connected data sources from SC actors. Connectivity tools include: intelligent adaptors such as translators to a common SCN data model; a publish/subscribe system for many-to-many communication of events with the ability to restrict who can subscribe to what data artefacts; and authentication and monitoring services. A single-sign-on federated-enabled authorisation system is provided for services or data sources, such that participants can deploy services via secure APIs, on the basis that SELIS is designed to support SOA and micro-services deployment for SCN-based applications.
2. Share aggregated data: allowing the creation of a shared situational picture linked to a knowledge graph and event log. Where appropriate, shared data from the event log is transferred to a blockchain ledger, thus increasing

trust levels on the use of the data with full traceability, auditability and immutability underpinning SC data transparency principles.

3. Optimise operations: through analysing the available aggregated data using the SELIS big data analytics module, offering generic analytics algorithms in the form of 'recipes' that can be easily configured to execute typical optimisation operations such as matching transport demand with available resources and route optimisation. Predictive and optimisation analytics can be also used to cover smart contracts associated with route and mode decisions in synchromodal transport.

Rapid implementation of SCNs is based on pre-built collaborative intelligence provided by configurable SELIS LCMs that are customised for specific logistics communities in global and regional SCs including last-mile distribution. SELIS has produced a library of models supporting European green logistics strategies (EGLS) that facilitate the composition of LCMs. An LCM service catalogue is used when setting up and configuring the connectivity semantics of the message broker by mapping LCMs to existing business semantics (participants, services, events, agreements). Importantly, LCM models use the currently existing standards for SCs and their data models and include WCO, UN/CEFACT, GS1 and UBL. SELIS liaises with the United Nations Centre for Trade Facilitation and Electronic Business (UN/CEFACT), drawing upon the vast experience and content available on international trade standards.

An important innovation is the use of knowledge graphs (KGs) to capture the SCN semantics based on relationships of entities relevant to a collaboration logistics model such as organisations, logistics objects/assets, resources and locations (Figure 6.3). KGs integrate spatial, business-social and temporal data. KGs are used to represent LCMs and provide the SC context to incorporate methods, services and tools to facilitate the better understanding and analyses of data. To this end, KGs support the efficient aggregation, ingestion and cleansing of data arriving from different sources, i.e. operational back end systems, databases, services and APIs, IoT controllers (e.g. joins, filtering, schema transformations, inferenced links creation in graphs of data and events).

The SELIS Cloud Infrastructure and Monitoring Platform supports monitoring (performance, scalability, usability) and security (encompassing the cloud platform security and identity management component). Important operational aspects such as SLA, uptime, high availability, network throughput and bandwidth are constantly monitored through the monitoring platform, which in turn provides early alerts in impending problems and orchestrates corrections if needed. The monitoring platform allows SCN operators and administrators to ensure that each SCN and the various infrastructures and services they depend upon are functioning correctly and performing well. As such, it provides an overall monitoring solution for one or more SCNs as an independent supervising platform and infrastructure monitoring entity to SCNs managed as a service.

The SELIS Project Methodology

The SELIS project methodology (Figure 6.3) combines a business and a technology innovation stream in creating the key elements of SCNs described earlier. Innovations are business-driven, capturing stakeholder needs, while at the same time exploring, exploiting and generating new ideas and ways to meet business metrics utilising the EGLSs. EGLSs can be applied in different stakeholder settings and focus on synchromodal transport involving rail, ship, barge, truck and terminal collaboration, as well as its application in urban and last-mile logistics.

The underlying concepts in SELIS approach include the following principal considerations:

1. In SELIS, all models and solutions have been tested in the SELIS Living Labs. Each Living Lab is connecting its community to at least one (primary) SCN and, per the Living Lab set-up, possibly to additional (secondary) SCNs for very active or organisationally extended community members, per (sub)community needs. The infrastructural SELIS components are composed in a set of coherent solutions, integrating best current open-source solutions, introducing SELIS innovative extensions for better configurability and easy deployment, considering the specific needs of the T&L domain. EGLS are strategies (e.g. synchromodal transport) supported by generic business models, used as guidance for the creation of a simulated environment, where collaboration solutions are tested and validated before being customised and implemented in real operational environments in the Living Labs.
2. The LCMs are composed for specific communities based on EGLS and logistics message exchange standards.
3. SCNs' ICT infrastructure comprises open-source software components that support logistics communities in implementing an LCM.
4. Each SELIS Living Lab sets up a stakeholder-centred ecosystem, for the systematic evaluation of innovative ideas and technological solutions in real-life use cases. Therefore, the Living Labs are evolving experiments for specific logistics communities, testing instantiations of LCMs. In the Living Labs the LCMs address the specific T&L community requirements, enabling the experimentation and testing of both business and technology innovations.
5. An SCN may include virtual subspaces for each Living Lab. Virtual spaces are created based on a 'cooperation agreement' that defines who will share, what nature and type of data, with whom under and what circumstances.
6. The messaging and communications based upon the pub/sub protocol is the vehicle to allow actors to publish and subscribe to data and events.
7. The KG in its simplest function is a service that acts as a database for storing historical facts and the current state of a SC. T&L applications can

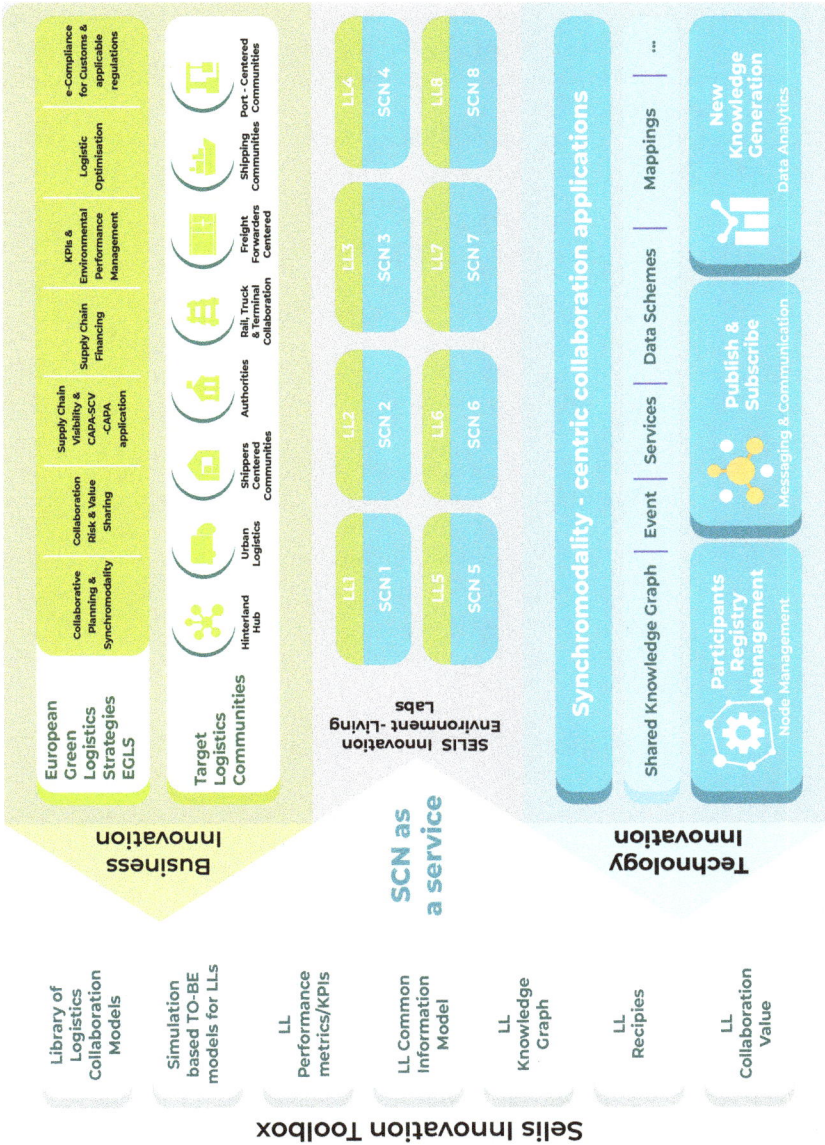

Figure 6.3: The SELIS research methodology.

query the KG and get insights on the state of the SC. The KG is also used for semantic data transformation and for the aggregation of data that is published from external and legacy systems.

8. An SCN incorporates a 'node controller' for node management, listening to events and populating the KG and data analytics. Deep learning techniques can then be used to discover new actors or refine relationships that also extend the KG.

9. The SCN data analytics enable complex analytics to furnish easy-to-understand business KPIs.

Collaboration Logistics Models (CLMs)

The SELIS Reference T&L Collaboration Framework

The SELIS Reference T&L Collaboration Framework (Figure 6.4) assumes that T&L communities are involved in three types of transport chains:

1. Global SCs characterised by a long shipping leg (and increasingly rail) and therefore important to deal efficiently with customs and other regulatory formalities.

2. Regional/continental SCs mainly linking manufacturers with regional retailers and increasingly a direct distribution of their products purchased from their own e-commerce channels.

3. Urban logistics and last-mile distribution, which are usually integrated with the previous two chains.

SCNs represent communities that can be linked to provide end-to-end SC ICT collaboration enablement, via solutions with reduced cost and improved environmental performance. A federation of SCNs can be used to support corridor-level collaboration and optimisation. Finally, inter-corridor collaboration will lead to collaborative networks towards realising the PI vision. The specific logistics community models developed in SELIS to support this are bound to the European green logistic strategies and capabilities, which are described in the following section.

SELIS EGLSs

The core rationale for EGLSs is that SC visibility enables SC performance management. Collaborative planning and synchromodal transport represents an operational strategy to improve performance (particularly environmental) by exploiting visibility through the synchronised deployment of logistics resources in a collaborative way.

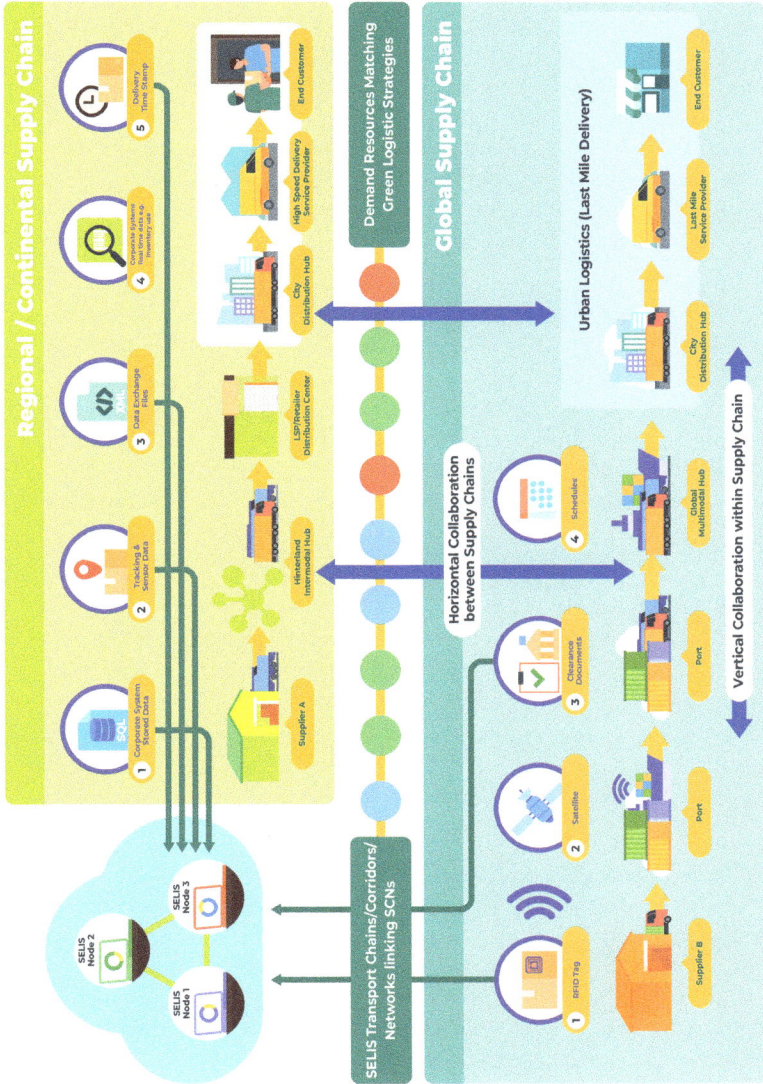

Figure 6.4: The SELIS T&L Collaboration Framework – high-level view.

SELIS EGLS descriptors

EGLS1: Collaborative planning and synchromodality. Depending on the specific context, there are different opportunities for collaboration, for sharing transportation capacity, warehousing capacity, aggregation of orders in the last-mile and innovative bundling at regional level. SELIS brings together approaches where infrastructure capacity is allocated to traffic flow, and where vehicle capacity is allocated to containers that need to be transported, and will support vertical integration of transport services (e.g. deep-sea transportation, terminal handling operations and land transportation).

EGLS2: Collaboration risk and value sharing between supply chain partners is gaining attention as a means to remedy sub-optimal logistics and yield significant business benefits such as inventory or cost reduction and improved asset utilisation. However, the lack of gain-sharing models defining the allocation of costs, investment, resources, benefits and risks between stakeholders are major barriers for the collaboration solutions (Eye for Transport 2010). Real-life operational data from SELIS community nodes allows greater transparency on collaboration by displaying KPIs to monitor in real time the business impacts of the collaboration and further refine compensation and risk-sharing rules.

EGLS3: Supply chain visibility and CAPA provide to supply chain players timely information for better decision support. The weakest link in supply chain visibility tends to be in transit status events at shipment level and in particular status updates about ocean shipments (GS1 2019). SELIS aims for end-to-end supply chain visibility (Titze & Barger 2015) delivering controlled access and transparency. SELIS solutions use a supply chain ontology–knowledge graph to link real-time information directly to KPIs improving visibility readiness.

EGLS4: Supply chain financing. The fundamental principle of SCF is that firms can decrease their cost of external financing by effectively tracking events in the physical supply chain and reliably disseminating this information to financial intermediaries in the capital markets. SELIS facilitates SCF solutions that rely on reliable dissemination of supply chain information. SELIS will also enable the promotion of green strategies through SCF programmes.

EGLS5: KPIs and Environmental Performance Management. According to the European Commission (2015b), transport decision makers are presently unable to benchmark available transport services with respect to GHG emissions and the importance of an accepted harmonised emission computation method has become stronger (Davydenko et al.

2014). The Global Logistics Emissions Council (GLEC) aims to create a universal way of calculating emissions (Smart Freight Centre 2019). The result has been the creation of the GLEC Framework to make carbon accounting work for industry.

EGLS6: Logistics optimisation. Previous research in supply chain optimisation has developed integrated models that typically seek to minimise the total production, inventory and distribution costs. An assumption is made with regard to the existence of an SCN acting as central controller/planner who is orchestrating the entire supply chain and has the authority to implement these optimisation strategies. SELIS extends approaches developed by Laporte (1992), Stahlbock and Voß (2008) and Crainic (2000) by including new collaboration synchromodality and visibility models.

EGLS7: e-compliance for customs. SELIS provides compliance solutions as component of integrated and 'smart' international supply chains, which in turn rely on new interoperability support standards and associated connectivity technologies. SELIS provides a technological solution that is based on the concept of using data pipeline principles to collect standardised supply chain data from as close as possible to their original sources, making higher-quality data available earlier to cross-border agency either directly or through the SELIS community node.

SELIS Target Logistics Communities (LCs)

SELIS target LCs represent market segments that will potentially be using similar types of supply chain community nodes, implying similar collaboration logistics models (CLMs).

SELIS LCs descriptors

Transport and logistics authorities. The main challenge for SELIS has been to establish a unified national and trans-border information exchange environment between private and public stakeholder groups, based on the European (DG TAXUD) alignment of regulatory requirements to the World Customs Organization Data Model as foreseen in the new Union Customs Code.

(Box continued on next page)

(Box continued from previous page)

Shippers- and retailer-centred communities. Shippers and large retailers, who have traditionally contracted 3PLs, are increasingly taking control of SCs by combining external and internal providers, leading to challenging 'collaborative spaces'; they are increasingly engaging in horizontal collaborations to form transportation and warehousing synergies. SELIS focused on SC collaborations aided by secure/privacy-preserving collaborative services, seeking to identify the key drivers of value chain efficiency across many players to drive end-to-end chain optimisation for a global maximum instead of local (e.g. single player optimisation).

Freight forwarders-centred communities. Freight forwarders (FF) search for opportunities to increase their efficiency and create competitive advantages. SELIS aims to increase FFs' insight into their customer's needs and behaviour and to facilitate horizontal collaborations with other logistics service providers, allowing better service quality, increased asset utilisation and economies of scale.

Port-centred communities. Ports are increasingly becoming a key facilitator for synchromodal transport and are expected to play a central role as smart hubs in PI networks. A port SCN can complement existing port community systems (PCSs) or can be used by smaller ports as an alternative to PCSs.

Shipping communities. An undeniable success factor for maritime transport is the seamless integration in intermodal transport chains, providing one-stop-shopping for transport shipping. SCNs improve interaction between ship and port, for optimised terminal resource planning and predictive port vicinity traffic.

Rail, truck and terminal network communities. Road–rail combined transport and transhipments are important for the sustainability of the EU logistics and transportation industry. SCNs support real-time information to allow coordinated slot planning, reduce the crane operations per loading unit, improve resources use and optimise trains use by minimising empty wagons travelling.

Hinterland hub communities. Current trends in maritime logistics often consider the presence of inland freight terminals, where goods are consolidated before shipment, such as hinterland hubs or dry ports. SELIS's focus is on facilitating synchromodality through the free flow of information between SCNs installed in inland hubs enabling flexible and dynamic routing strategies and operational support.

Urban logistics communities. Urban logistics is characterised by defragmented deliveries, important external constraints (e.g. access-restricted areas, congestion, lack of appropriate unloading infrastructure), and significant environmental and economic externalities. SCNs support urban logistics collaboration and information sharing models, as well as the vehicle to infrastructure architecture, and real-time sensor data consolidation and management, to improve the last-mile delivery visibility and environmental performance

---

Developing Collaborative Logistics Models

Figure 6.5 shows the main steps towards developing an LCM.

Step 1 involves modelling the SCN community's data sharing needs, using an informal or ad hoc (schema-free) notation, e.g. a graph.

Step 2 involves formalising the shared data model using one of the industry standards that the SCN community agrees upon, e.g. GS1 and UBL. The specification of any necessary adapters to support conversion between data schemas by SCN is also carried out at this stage.

Step 3 is where the main collaboration use cases are identified and modelled, in order to identify any inconsistencies and gaps in the data modelling activities of the first step.

STEP 1
Create LCM Data Models from Community Goals

STEP 4
Map EGLS to Standard Processes & Information Exchanges

STEP 2
Get standards for Processes & Information Exchanges

STEP 3
Refine Models based on collaboration Use Case descriptions

Figure 6.5: Steps for LCM development.

Step 4 is where the EGLS data requirements are mapped to the shared data model of step 3. From that, the specifications for configuring the various components and subsystems of SCN such as the big data analytics can be derived, as explained in the previous section. Such specifications comprise a configuration script that the SCN administrator can run in order to obtain an instance of SCN.

Information Exchange Models, Semantics and Knowledge Graphs

The SELIS SCN supports a flexible data schema coupled with the execution of specific algorithms. SCN administrators have the ability to define upon node creation (i.e. during the node bootstrapping process) the abstract extensible data model they expect the SCN to support, according to the specific SCN data needs. In essence, to enable extensibility, SELIS identifies two types of data, according to the way it is updated/ingested, namely static and streaming data. Static data (or master data) consists of information that is not expected to change over time and defines specific SCN information.

In the SELIS case, the static information is grouped into 'entities'. Example of entities can be a track/vessel/train fleet, a list of stations/terminals/warehouses, etc. Static data is being ingested upon node bootstrapping. Streaming data consists of the information that changes over time, and in essence contains the messages that are exchanged between the SELIS participating entities. Message content (e.g. GPS traces, IoT and controller device readings, proof of deliveries) are stored in an append-only data structure backed up by a highly efficient distributed data store that supports high-rate insertions/updates.

The data structure capturing the real-world events is the event log, which captures all the operational data that is exchanged between SCN participants in the form of messages. The data model that is the combination of entities and event log defines a typical star schema approach found in datamarts and it is being used to perform the execution of the analytics algorithms (i.e. the SELIS recipes). Both the schema and the recipes are explicitly defined and configured upon node creation, utilising an easy-to-use API coupled with a comprehensive GUI. Any relations between the entities are captured in the KG, whereas the entity/event log schema facilitates the execution of analytics recipes.

The SELIS tools support the integration of the common information exchange models and metamodels and provides mapping functionality so as to enable cross-schema mapping. Further, it has the capability to create the necessary web services components and deploy the developed connectivity components as micro-services in the SCN.

All defined concepts inserted in the SELIS models may be exported, stored, enhanced and accessed in a graph database, thereby interacting with the SELIS KGs content database. This results in a powerful analysis and homogenisation environment, where, by implementing specific algorithms and queries, it is possible to introduce additional semantic content to the nodes, to further enhance and enrich the modelled information on the SC and transportation. A semi-automatic mapping tool developed can usefully assist the mapping process in the information exchanges. This tool has been enriched to include content information by integrating properly the standard data types, consolidating with the existing common information exchanges' data model structures.

The use of SC ontologies in message transformations via semantic gateways has been specified and is exemplified in related projects, such as the e-Freight project, in iCargo, and in CORE. Most of the work in ontologies has been based in the LogiCO, which explicitly specifies the main concepts adopted in the logistics domain and LogiServ. The main idea is to use LogiCO as a bridging ontology to map and transform from other ontologies developed, i.e. WCO, UN/CEFACT, GS1, NIEM etc. The SELIS semi-automatic mapping tool is using and extending this approach, by running multiple ontologies to assist mapping.

SELIS Generic Applications and Results from Living Labs

A reference domain model of the seven sub-domains has been produced, as shown in Figure 6.6. This model has been implemented as a number of business models that provide a starting point for creating SC applications in the context of SELIS and beyond. This functionality was provided to the Living Labs stakeholders via a number of application dashboards, such as the stock optimisation dashboard, the barge ETA dashboard and the shipment tracking dashboard.

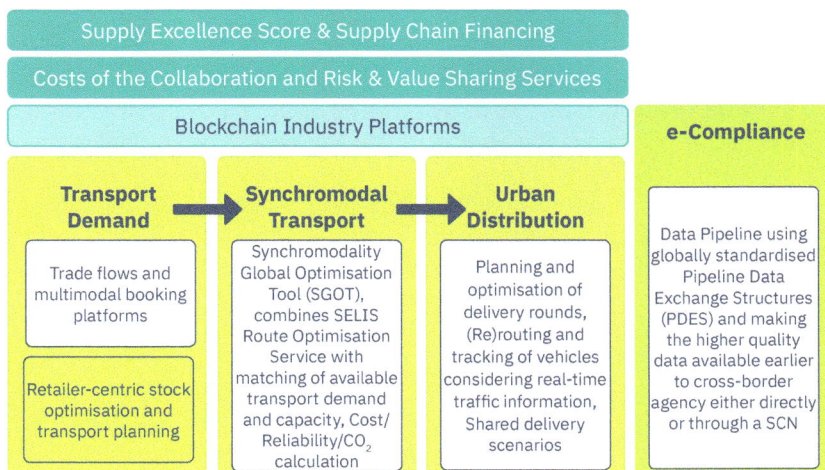

			e-Compliance
Supply Excellence Score & Supply Chain Financing			
Costs of the Collaboration and Risk & Value Sharing Services			
Blockchain Industry Platforms			
Transport Demand	**Synchromodal Transport**	**Urban Distribution**	
Trade flows and multimodal booking platforms	Synchromodality Global Optimisation Tool (SGOT), combines SELIS Route Optimisation Service with matching of available transport demand and capacity, Cost/ Reliability/CO_2 calculation	Planning and optimisation of delivery rounds, (Re)routing and tracking of vehicles considering real-time traffic information, Shared delivery scenarios	Data Pipeline using globally standardised Pipeline Data Exchange Structures (PDES) and making the higher quality data available earlier to cross-border agency either directly or through a SCN
Retailer-centric stock optimisation and transport planning			

Figure 6.6: SELIS Applications Framework.

Conclusions

The SELIS project has produced key enablers towards a Shared European Logistics Intelligent Information Space with a focus on synchromodality. SELIS supply chain community nodes enable smart collaboration between stakeholders along the transport chain based on information sharing about all available transport modalities in real time in order to switch between transport modes (water, rail and road) in the most effective and environmentally friendly way.

SELIS has developed and demonstrated how connectivity tools can be integrated with security and privacy-preserving services to enable data-driven collaboration models that result in substantial economic and environmental benefits for a broad range of T&L communities. It has highlighted the importance of specifying logistics collaboration models as an innovation engine and how these models can be used to configure the supply chain community nodes. Central to the SELIS approach and architecture is using big data analytics to establish predictive and optimisation algorithms that provide business value to SCN participants. The design of the SCN comprises the use of shared knowledge graphs to manage interactions of logistics collaboration actors, advanced semantics, security, and analytics components with integrated content based routing that constitute two early patent filings (already awarded in France). At the same time, making these components open source guarantees broader use by European researchers and industry. The later three patent filings on cooperative stock optimisation for integrated SC management, intelligent dynamic container routing and smart contracts reflect the project's vision towards realising a next level of automation in synchromodality in the direction of PI through SCN federation.

From the outset, the importance of synchromodality and strategic capabilities such as SC visibility to support its implementation was well understood and a main workstream was dedicated in this area. This produced a valuable library of models, called EGLSs. It is, however, recognised that real value from this work will come from industry acceptance, use and extension/refinement of these models. Consolidation and governance of logistics collaboration models for efficient low-carbon transport are flagged as important actions for industry forums such as ALICE and standardisation bodies such as UN/CEFACT, with whom SELIS collaborated in a productive way.

In terms of future research, the project experience points to the need for extending the community models tested in the Living Labs as well as in other projects. Classification of collaboration models is needed and further elaboration to reflect different communities' needs in the light of emerging transport innovations such as electric and autonomous vehicles and IoT driven automation as well as infrastructure developments, aligning the innovation road maps across different modes (Figure 6.7).

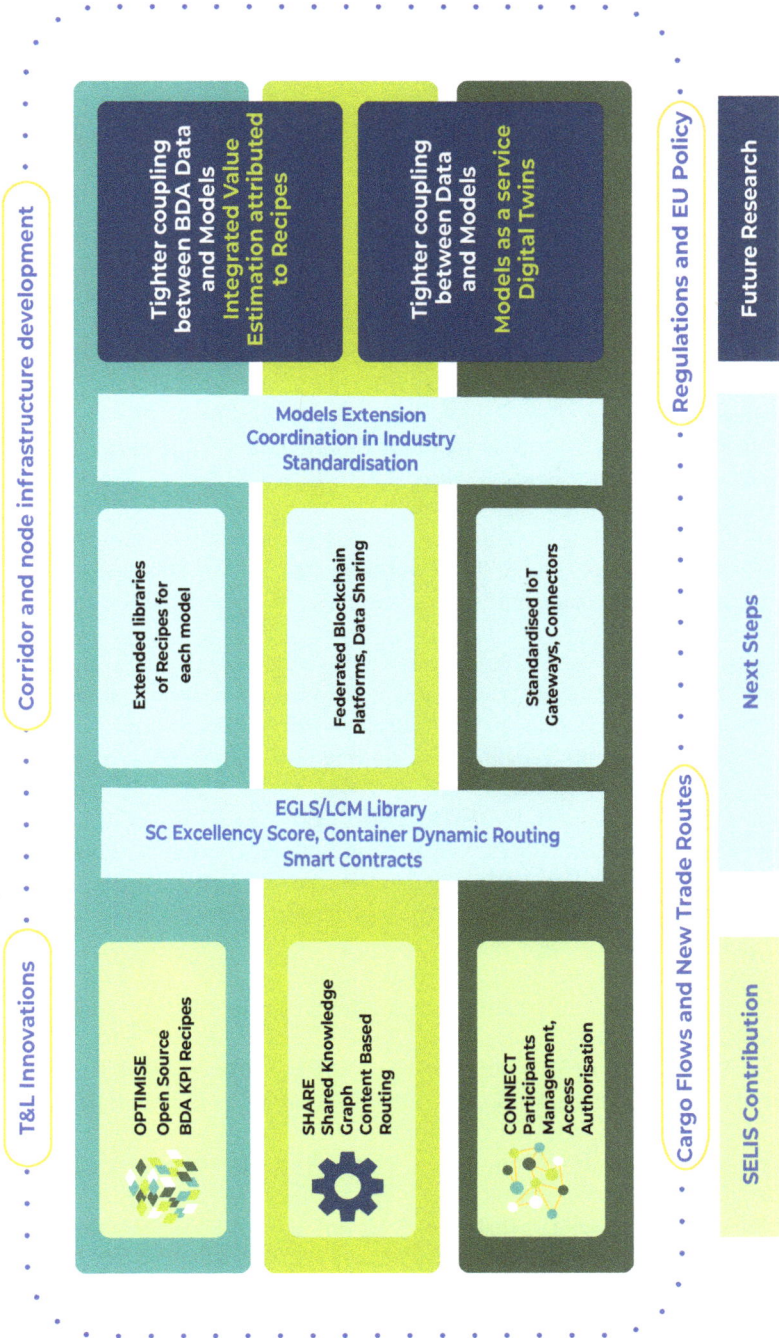

Figure 6.7: Alignment of innovation road maps across different modes.

References

ALICE. (2016). Alliance for Logistic Innovation through Collaboration in Europe. Retrieved from: http://www.etp-logistics.e; http://www.etp-logistics.eu/?p=1298.

Christopher, M. (2016). *Logistics & supply chain management.* Pearson UK, London.

Clausen, U., De Bock, J. & Lu, M. (2016). Logistics trends, challenges, and needs for further research and innovation. In Lu, M. and De Bock, J. (eds), *Sustainable logistics and supply chains,* (pp. 1–13). Springer International Publishing, Cham.

Crainic, T. G. (2000). Service network design in freight transportation. *EU Journal of Operational Research, 122*(2), 288.

Davydenko, I., Ehrler, V., de Ree, D., Lewis, A. & Tavasszy, L. (2014). Towards a global CO2 calculation standard for supply chains: Suggestions for methodological improvements. *Transportation Research Part D: Transport and Environment, 32,* 362–372.

DTLF. (2018). Enabling organisations to reap the benefits of data sharing in logistics and supply chain. Retrieved from: http://www.dtlf.eu/sites/default/files/public/uploads/fields/page/field_file/executive_summary2_reading__0.pdf.

European Commission. (2015a). Smart and sustainable logistics for a competitive Europe. Retrieved from: http://www.transport-research.info/Upload/Documents/201504/20150430_162337_40619_PB08_fin.pdf.

European Commission. (2015b). Fact-finding studies for an EU strategy for freight transport logistics, Lot 3: Introduction of a standardised carbon footprint methodology, FV355/2012/MOVE/D1/ETU/SI2.659384.

European Commission. (2015c). Common communication and navigation platforms for pan-European logistics applications. Retrieved from: https://ec.europa.eu/info/funding-tenders/opportunities/portal/screen/opportunities/topic-details/mg-6.3-2015.

European Commission. (2019). Digital Transport and Logistics Forum. Retrieved from: https://www.digitaltransport.eu/2019/pages/sessions-description.

Eye for Transport. (2010). European Supply Chain Horizontal Collaboration.

Fawcett, S.E., McCarter, M.W., Fawcett, A.M., Webb, G.S. & Magnan, G.M., (2015). Why supply chain collaboration fails: the socio-structural view of resistance to relational strategies. *Supply Chain Management: An International Journal, 20*(6), 648–663.

Geissbauer, R., Roussel, J., Schrauf, S. & Strom, M. A. (2013). Next-generation supply chains. Efficient, fast and tailored. PWC Global SC Survey.

GS1. (2019). Supply Chain Visibility – A Critical Strategy to Optimize Cost and Service. Retrieved from: http://www.gs1.org/docs/visibility/Supply_Chain_Visibility_Aberdeen_Report.pdf.

Laporte, G. (1992). The vehicle routing problem: An overview of exact and approximate algorithms. *Journal of Operational Research, 59*(3), 345–358.

Leinbach, T. R. (2007). *Globalised freight transport: Intermodality, e-commerce, logistics and sustainability.* Edward Elgar Publishing, London.

McKinsey. (2021). Overcoming barriers to multitier supplier collaboration, Retrieved from: https://www.mckinsey.com/business-functions/operations /our-insights/overcoming-barriers-to-multitier-supplier-collaboration [accessed 7 July 2021].

Manners-Bell, J. (2016). *Introduction to global logistics: Delivering the goods.* Kogan Page Publishers, London.

OASIS. (2019). Oasis standards. Retrieved from: https://www.oasis-open.org /standards#ublv2.1.

PWC. (2019). Shifting patterns: The future of the logistics industry. Retrieved from: http://www.pwc.com/sg/en/publications/assets/future-of-the-logistics -industry.pdf.

Savy, M. (2016). Logistics as a political issue. *Transport Reviews, 36,* 413–417.

Simmer, L., Pfoser, S., Grabner, M., Schauer, O. & Putz, L.M. (2017). From horizontal collaboration to the physical internet – A case study from Austria. *International Journal of Transport Development and Integration, 1*(2), 129–136.

Smart Freight Centre. (2019). What is the GLEC Framework? Retrieved from: https://www.smartfreightcentre.org/en/how-to-implement-items/what-is -glec-framework/58.

Stahlbock, R. & Voß, S. (2008). Operations research at container terminals: A literature update. *OR Spectrum, 30*(1), 1–52.

Titze, C. & Barger Jr, R. (2015). Evolving concepts in supply chain. Gartner, January 2015.

UN Centre for Trade Facilitation and e-Business (UNECE). (2019a). UN/ CEFACT. Retrieved from: www.unece.org/cefact.html.

UNECE. (2019b). UN/CEFACT datatype catalogue. Retrieved from: https:// www.unece.org/cefact/codesfortrade/ccts_datatypecatalogue.html.

UNECE. (2019b). UN/CEFACT Core Component Library (CCL). Retrieved from: https://www.unece.org/cefact/codesfortrade/unccl/ccl_index.html.

World Bank. (2014). Logistics performance index: Connecting to compete 2014. LPI_Report_2014.

World Customs Organisation. (2019). WCO Data Model: Single window data harmonisation. Retrieved from: http://www.wcoomd.org/en/search.aspx ?keyword=tools_data+model.

CHAPTER 7

A Primer on Supply Chain Digital Transformation

Yingli Wang and Stephen Pettit

Digital Transformation

In the preceding chapters of this monograph, a range of approaches to digitalisation on aspects of supply chain activities have been considered. In conclusion, therefore, it is worth reflecting on what digital supply chain transformation for the supply chain means, and what the key developments in the near future are likely to be.

Digital transformation aims to improve an organisation's activities by triggering significant changes through a combination of information, computing, communication, and connectivity technologies (Vial 2019). It has been referred to as 'corporate initiatives to use the new capabilities afforded by digital technologies to transform the strategies and operations of organisations' (Li 2020: 810). Such changes do not necessarily, however, have to be organisation-centric and could be stimulated by changes that take place at either an industrial or a societal level. Thus, an organisation may need to

---

How to cite this book chapter:
Wang, Y., and Pettit, S. 2022. A Primer on Supply Chain Digital Transformation. In: Wang, Y., and Pettit, S. (eds.) *Digital Supply Chain Transformation: Emerging Technologies for Sustainable Growth*. Pp. 121–139. Cardiff: Cardiff University Press. DOI: https://doi.org/10.18573/book8.g. Licence: CC-BY-NC-ND 4.0

respond to changes taking place at one, or both, of those levels in order to remain competitive. However, whether they are leading in developing and implementing such changes or whether they are following the changes, the expected outcome would be that improvements in performance are seen across an organisation, resulting in improved levels of performance and competitive behaviour.

Digital technologies are a key source of disruption within the supply chain and a range of outcomes can be seen. Over the last decade, digitalisation has had a significant impact in altering consumer behaviour and expectations, both raising standards and lowering costs. It is now, for example, not uncommon for goods to be supplied to the consumer within 24 hours of an order being placed, sometimes even on the same day. The competitive landscape has thus been disrupted and traditional approaches to service provision have changed beyond recognition. Organisations that have been able to leverage digital platforms have faced lower barriers to entry into the market, for example not having to invest in traditional high street sales outlets, and have thus been able to combine products and services in different ways in order to generate new forms of digital offering. All of these have reduced the competitive advantage of incumbent players and hindered their sustainability. The increasing availability of data and the use of sophisticated algorithms to analyse and manipulate that data mean that organisations can target their customer base far more effectively.

Digitalisation also allows for the creation of new value propositions. An example of this is Netflix, whose business model was originally based on the rental of movies stored on physical media. Over the years, however, Netflix has moved away from this value proposition to become the first large-scale provider of video streaming services. More recently, it has leveraged data collected from the use of its streaming services to better understand the types of content its viewers enjoy, as well as how it is consumed, in order to help with the production of its own programming (Günther et al. 2017).

Digital transformation is a relatively new concept and is both complex and challenging. A 2018 McKinsey survey of 1,793 participants identified that only 16% of respondents said their organisations' digital transformations have successfully improved performance and also equipped them to sustain changes in the long term. An additional 7% said that performance improved but that those improvements were not sustained (Boutetière, Montagner & Reich 2018). This calls for a holistic approach to strategy and execution, moving away from disconnected digital experiments. The same survey identified that leadership, capability building, empowering workers, upgrading tools, and communication are critical success factors in any digital transformation initiatives.

Supply Chain Digital Transformation

The key question in any digital transformation strategy is: how can data and digital capabilities be used to create new value for existing and new customers? Chapter 1 briefly considered what digital transformation means in the supply chain context and proposed the use of a supply chain digital transformation value framework (Figure 1.2) to guide the design and execution of digital initiatives. In this context, it can be asserted that the value proposition, i.e. the question of what customer needs the business model will address, should be the primary driver of any supply chain digital transformation. Digital technology is a means to achieve supply chain goals but not an end of digital transformation itself. As rightfully stated by Tekic and Koroteev (2019), 'digital technology is the tastiest ingredient needed for making a digital transformation cake, while the business model is a master recipe for making the cake. If either of these two – the key ingredient or the recipe – is not optimal, the cake will not be worth serving' (p. 685).

With the framework in Chapter 1 as the starting point, we articulate further in this chapter how companies should leverage digital technologies in a systematic approach to gain competitive advantages, create value and produce desirable sustainable outcomes.

Where Do You Start?

In recent years, there has been a significant amount of hype around digital transformation, promoting the potential benefits of such change. However, many supply chain executives are overwhelmed with the complexity and diversity of instigating such changes, and struggle to identify, understand and evaluate the strategic options for their supply chains. To fully leverage the potential of digital technologies, supply chain executives need to be able to make sense of the digital landscape and equip themselves with sufficient understanding about digital technology capabilities and trajectories, and thus put themselves in a position to be able to envision the possibilities of potential applications for transforming their supply chains. This means that supply chain leaders need to become 'digital translators' (Wang et al. 2021) or 'visionaries' (Hartley and Sawaya 2019) who understand how technologies work, can intermediate between the physical supply chain and information technology, and possess excellent change management skills.

Being able to see and understand the realm of possibilities afforded by digital technology is one of the two pillars that set the foundation of successful supply chain digital transition (see Figure 7.1). The second pillar relates to aligning the understanding of technology with business and supply chain strategies.

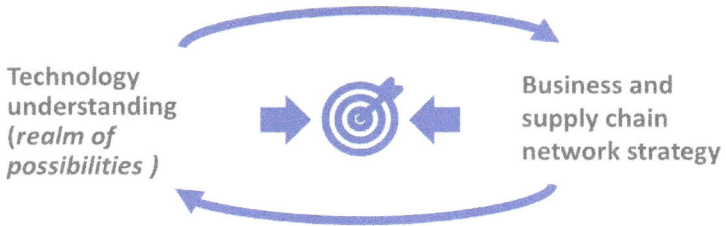

Technology understanding (*realm of possibilities*)

Business and supply chain network strategy

Figure 7.1: Two pillars for digitalising supply chain. Source: Authors.

By aligning the two pillars, companies can develop a clearly defined, coherent digital supply chain strategy that fully integrates with their business and supply chain strategies.

Top Leadership Commitment and Support

Once companies have developed a well-articulated supply chain digital strategy, they will need to fully commit to it. Lack of leadership support is one of the major roadblocks for successful supply chain digital transformation. CEOs need to sponsor the programme heavily, the executive board will need to appoint dedicated senior executives to take ownership of the transformation, and the management team will need to ensure collaboration internally between the different functions, and externally with suppliers, customers and other supply chain stakeholders.

When people in key roles (both the senior leaders of the organisation and those in transformation-specific roles) are more involved in digital transformation, success, although not guaranteed, is more likely. They will be instrumental in setting a high level of aspiration, fostering a sense of urgency for transformation, and establishing a clear change strategy to execute the vision. Having an astute digital leader (e.g. chief digital officer) has also been identified as one of the keys to transformation success (Boutetière, Montagner & Reich 2018).

More importantly, senior leaders should *lead by example*, i.e. they express by their actions a set of values and beliefs to which they want their followers to subscribe (House 1977). Put simply, if leaders want to empower employees to have the shared ownership and pride in digital transformation, they themselves have to model the way, personally embrace the change and provide a live demonstration of how things should be done, and communicate why things should be done. This type of leadership can thus have a cascading effect and instils a behavioural stimulus that motivates employees to invest their own resources and engage more fully with the digital transformation programme (Eldor 2021).

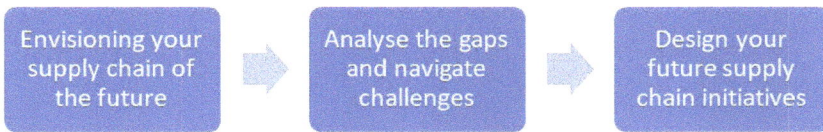

Figure 7.2: Three steps to translate strategy into action. Source: Authors.

Translating the Strategy into Action

There are different approaches to operationalising the strategy into action. Here, a simple three-step approach is proposed (Figure 7.2). Many digital transformation initiatives start by identifying the problematic areas (often known as 'pain points') in supply chains and try to utilise digital technologies to address those pain points. Though this is a valid approach, it can be argued that it may bear more fruitful outcomes if supply chain executives start by first envisioning what future supply chains would look like in their own industrial context. This approach is inspired by the foresight–insight–action model developed by the Institute for the Future (Johansen 2020).

Linking back to Chapter 1, which identified the key characteristics of a future supply chain, a vision of what an organisation's future supply chain would look like can be created. For instance, it can be envisaged that future supply chains will increasingly become not just more automated but more autonomous.

Next, working backwards, there is a need to understand the state of the current supply chain, and ask how transformation from an 'as-is' state to the desirable 'to-be' state can be achieved. By doing this, there is a need to start examining the gaps that exist between the current and future state of the sector and understand what the potential challenges and barriers in the transformation journey are. This is where the existing pain points are discovered that must be resolved in order to realise the vision for future. For instance, following the future vision of an autonomous supply chain, it might be found that the existing supply chain has issues such as siloed IT systems, lack of end-to-end supply chain visibility and a lack of data scientists in developing AI algorithms for supply chain planning.

In step 2, it is necessary to emphasise the importance of knowing the current digital capability and maturity of an organisation. The work of Bonnet and Westerman (2021) on digital capability offers a useful framework to assess current digital capabilities. Although the framework is not specific to supply chain digital transformation, it nonetheless serves as a guide for benchmarking and self-assessment. They propose how to examine an organisation's digital capability from the following perspective:

1. business model: digital enhancements; information-based service extensions and multi-sided platform businesses;

2. customer experience: experience design, customer intelligence and emotional engagement;
3. operations: core process automation, connected and dynamic operations and data-driven decision-making;
4. employee experience: augmentation; future-readying and flex-forcing (agile sourcing of talent);
5. digital platform: organisational digital backbone, external facing platform connecting to customers and ecosystem partners, data platform for intense analytics and AI deployment.

The third step is to explore how the identified gaps, while taking consideration of legacy constraints and challenges, can be addressed. The output could be a digital road map that defines different supply chain scenarios, develops goals and objectives, and establishes initiatives and deployment solutions. Digital initiatives that can be put into place could include real-time supply chain tracking, robotic process automation, data lake and master data management, supply chain digital twinning, prescriptive supply chain planning, etc. A road map not only defines a portfolio of digital initiatives but also needs to create initiative measurement criteria and key performance indicators (KPIs).

Supply chain digital transformation tends to consume significant resources, and many initiatives observed in practice takes several years if not longer to complete, ranging from investing in supply chain visibility, setting up control towers, AI-enabled supply chain planning and demand forecasting to onboarding suppliers digitally. The complexities induced by such changes can be overwhelming and affect many parts of a supply chain. A road map helps organisations to navigate complexities, make more informed decisions, and align stakeholders to stay on track to reach their desirable future state. However, a cautionary approach needs to be taken, understanding that with a road map there is a risk that organisations focus too much on the technology rather than how to best achieve supply chain goals. Thus, it is strongly recommended that the value framework developed in Chapter 1 is used in combination with a road map so as not to lose oversight of the transformation process.

Approaches to Supply Chain Digital Transformation

Typically, there are two primary approaches of digitalisation, often referred to as digital 'ambidexterity': (1) exploitation – optimising and enhancing existing supply chain operations – and (2) exploration – launching new business and supply chain models. While the former tends to lead to productivity gains and cost cutting, the latter is associated with business growth and revenue generation, albeit with a higher risk of failure. When an organisation begins to think about undergoing a transformation, it is crucial to balance between the two and allocate resources carefully.

Based on current research, with a group of global digital champions at the forefront of digital transformation, including Amazon, Alibaba, Baidu, Google, JD.com, Uber, VMWare and Slack, Li (2020) found that at least three new approaches are emerging in those leading organisations. They are: (1) innovating by experimenting, (2) radical transformation via successive incremental changes and (3) dynamic sustainable advantages through an evolving portfolio of temporary advantages. Those approaches challenge traditional linear approaches for leading digital transformation and highlight the need for new and iterative approaches for bridging the strategy–execution gap in the volatile digital economy. The author suggested an agile approach to try out many new ideas and select the successful ones to scale up rapidly. By breaking up large-scale, radical digital transformation into smaller, more manageable strategic investments, organisations are able to experiment with many new ideas based on rapid piloting and scaling. Given the rapid changing digital landscape, competitive advantages can no longer be sustained for long periods. Therefore, it is advisable that companies pursue successive temporary advantages via its evolving portfolio of digital initiatives. The cumulative effect can be significant over time.

For supply chain organisations, their businesses are not the digital native ones as discussed in Li's work. There will be more constraints to experiment with new ideas simultaneously and scale up is more complicated because physical supply chain structures and processes need to be taken into consideration. However, the underlying principles are observed and applicable in traditional incumbent organisations too. For inspiration, incumbents can still learn from those companies born digital. In fact, a white paper published by the World Economic Forum (WEF) (2017) put forward similar arguments for manufacturers that speed and agility in adopting digital technology is the defining factor for digital transformation, and emphasised the importance of experiments ('fail fast, fail early' mindset), organisation alignment and level of integration (e.g. via a collaborative network of partners). A further report by the WEF (2018), via a cross-sector analysis, proposed five key enablers and four underlying execution principles for maximising returns on digital investment (Figure 7.3). These offer valuable insights for supply chain leaders when they try to jump-start their digital journey.

A Digital Transformation Framework for Supply Chain Leaders

While there has been a plethora of studies proposing guiding principles and recommendations about digital transformation, there has been a lack of supply chain-specific frameworks to guide actions in practice. It is suggested that using the three pillars as shown in Figure 7.4 – data and technology, people, and process – will provide a viable way forward. Change management is at the centre of the three pillars as it is a key instrument and process for realising digital transformation.

Key Enablers			
2. Forward-looking skills agenda Workforce digital mindset; innovation the focus of training		**3. Ecosystem thinking** Collaborating within the value chain (e.g., with suppliers, distributors etc.)	
	1. **Agile and digital-savvy leadership** Strategic vision, purpose, skills, intent and alignment across management		
4. Data Access and Management Strong data infrastructure and warehouse capability combined with the right analytics and communication tools		**5. Technology infrastructure readiness** Building required technology infrastructure to ensure strong cloud capabilities, cybersecurity and interoperability	
Execution Principles			
Establish clear ownership of digital investment	Invest in use-cases, not technologies	Fail fast, fail cheap	Follow an outcome-based approach

Figure 7.3: Key enablers and execution principles for maximising returns on digital investment. Source: Based on WEF (2018).

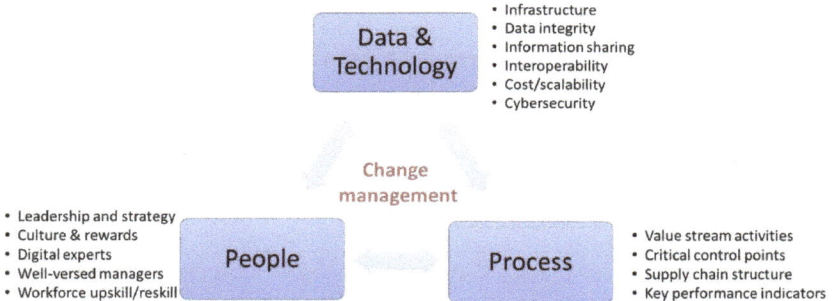

Figure 7.4: A framework for supply chain digital transformation. Source: Authors.

Data and technology

The availability of huge amounts of data (structured and unstructured) gives rise to the concept of the digital economy. Data is now increasingly recognised by firms to be a significant asset to deliver market-driven innovations such as personalised products/services, real-time supply chain tracking and risk alerts, predictive maintenance and advanced demand sensing and forecasting.

With the increasing power of data, the importance of data integrity cannot be overstated. Without ensuring data integrity, the usefulness of data becomes diminished as any information extracted from it is not reliable for accurate decision-making. Many people would confuse *data integrity* with *data quality*, but the former encapsulates multiple perspectives and refers to the reliability, completeness and authenticity of data. In a scenario where an advanced machine learning (ML) algorithm for supply chain planning has been built, if the data being fed into the ML model is inaccurate, inconsistent, incomplete and dated, the outputs will be inaccurate. In practice, many firms struggle to capture the right data in the right format for them to be available for deployment to big data analytics and AI algorithms. It is not uncommon to see many organisations spend a great deal of time and effort in cleaning and preparing data before putting it into a 'data lake'[6] for analytics consumption. The point of a data lake is that its simplicity enables broad, flexible and unbiased data exploration and discovery via advanced forms of analytics (such as data mining, statistics and machine learning) (Russom 2021).

To acquire the required data, an organisation needs the correct digital infrastructure. This typically includes hardware, software and data platforms. For instance, if a firm wants to build digital capability for end-to-end real-time supply chain visibility, it will have to consider automatic data capturing technologies such as the internet of things (IoT) devices, wireless communication networks such as Wi-Fi 6 or 5G and cloud computing platforms for processing the collected data. A key question supply chain leaders should ask is 'how digital are my core processes?' (e.g. procurement, operations, customer engagement and logistics).

Another important issue is cybersecurity. With supply chains becoming increasingly digital and the rise of cybercrime- and cyber-enabled information operations, there is an urgent need to build cyber resilience into supply chains. According to the UK's National Cyber Security Centre (NCSC 2018), information theft is the fastest-rising consequence of cybercrime. Other cybercrime trends in the supply chain space include cyber criminals targeting the vulnerabilities of IoT devices and of third- or fourth-party supply chain partners' digital infrastructure to gain entry to target systems. Instead of asking what cyberattacks might be possible on computer systems, supply chain leaders need to ask how a cyberattack could disrupt their supply chain (Parenty & Domet 2019). Companies should identify their critical supply chain activities, assess the risks to those activities, and then identify the systems supporting them. Intervention measures should then be put into place to reduce those systems' vulnerability.

Other key issues to consider include the cost of deploying digital technologies, interoperability issues between different information systems within and across organisations, and how the focal company should share information (what to share via which means) with supply chain ecosystem partners.

---

[6] A data lake is a concept consisting of a collection of storage instances of various data assets. These assets are stored in a near-exact, or even exact, copy of the source format and are in addition to the originating data stores (Russom 2021).

People

The people pillar broadly incorporates the 'soft' issues such as leadership and strategy, skills, culture and behavioural change, as well as reward schemes. Having digitally aware supply chain leaders, a workforce with sufficient digital literacy and digital experts such as data scientists in place will give companies a competitive edge to their digitalisation journey. Data science skills and roles, although only forming a relatively small part of the workforce, are in particularly high demand across all sectors (WEF 2019).

Skills

Digital transformation needs to be accompanied by appropriate investment in talent and workforce reskilling and upscaling. Workforce reskilling and upskilling should not be treated as a one-off investment but a continuous process in order to respond to fast-changing technologies and associated skills demand. Wang, Skeete and Owusu (2021), when investigating the application of AI in process automation, identified that, if employees do not possess the appropriate skills and knowledge of how the AI system works, they will create unnecessary workarounds within a system and compromise its intended effectiveness. Fortunately, many firms now realise the urgency of digital talent development and have launched initiatives such as digital academies to prepare their workforce for the digital world.

For instance, Schneider Electric (SE), a leading manufacturer in energy and industry automation, has developed a 'digital citizenship programme', aiming to upskill over 90% of its employees (SE 2020). The programme covers essential future skills including data science, digital economy and digital technologies, as well as cybersecurity. SE also set up a supply chain academy creating its own curriculum focusing heavily on data science, analytics and robotic process automation. The energy company Equinor (formerly Statoil) created its 'Digital Academy' to increase digital literacy and capabilities across all levels of the organisation (WEF 2018). Through the programme, the company launched various initiatives. For instance, it introduced a 'digital word of the week' to raise awareness and interest, established a Yammer (social networking) group to share knowledge and create engagement, and invited people to become digital ninjas, training them in 'digital ninja gyms' and making those digital ninjas the ambassadors to drive the digital agenda.

Culture and Behavioural Changes

Leadership is critical but transformation success depends more on the way people on the front lines implement new digital tools (Leonardi 2020). Digital transformation requires a digital culture that supports this change. Digital culture in organisations is a set of shared assumptions and understanding about an organisation functioning in a digital context (Martínez-Caro, Cegarra-Navarro & Alfonso-Ruiz 2020). Cultural change underpins the sustainability of the impact generated by digital transformation. Adopting a digital organisational culture will provide employees with not only the right tools but also the right structures, incentives and mindsets to integrate new technologies into their work.

However, cultural and behavioural change is perceived by many to be the biggest challenge for a successful digital transformation (Buvat et al. 2018; Catlin et al. 2017). Culture is a complex and intangible 'thing' and it is difficult to know where to start and how to create an organisational culture that is fit for digital transformation. Katzenbach, Steffen and Kronley (2012) suggested that focusing on changing just a few critical behaviours to break through organisational inertia, while honouring their organisation's culture strength, will mean that culture can be an accelerator of change, rather than an impediment. In a similar vein, Mesaglio, Olding and Ommeren (2019) suggested the use of small but powerful culture hacks to find vulnerable points in an organisation's culture and turn them in to real change that sticks. Struckman et al. (2020) proposed a three-step methodology to change culture: (1) define the North Star of how you want your organisational members to behave using culture attributes. Make sure the North Star of behaviours makes sense given the business strategy. (2) Describe the shifts in both mindset and behaviours that create understanding about the extent of the behaviour changes using a from/to/because model. (3) Create an action plan to change the behaviours described in the from/to/because model by changing the systems, processes and practices that reinforce the old behaviours. Another useful resource is the digital culture guidebook produced by the WEF (2021), which articulates four pillars of digital culture (collaborative, data-driven, customer-centric and innovative) and prescribes detailed guidance on how to accelerate digital culture.

Behavioural research is receiving increased attention in various academic disciplines. A method that has recently come to prominence in the last decade to influence behaviour change is nudge theory, developed by Richard Thaler[7] and Cass Sunstein in 2008. Nudge theory is based upon the idea that, by shaping the environment, also known as the choice architecture, one can influence the likelihood that one option is chosen over another by individuals. A key factor of nudge theory is the ability for an individual to maintain freedom of choice and to feel in control of the decisions they make. An example of such a nudge is switching the placement of junk food in a store, so that fruit and other healthy options are located next to the cash register, while junk food is relocated to another part of the store. Currently, the use of nudge theory to drive desirable supply chain behaviours for digital transformation is an underexplored area but it may produce fruitful results if done well.

---

[7] Richard Thaler won the Sveriges Riksbank Prize in Economic Sciences in Memory of Alfred Nobel 2017 for his contributions to behavioural economics.

Process

Supply chain transformation requires a baseline understanding of the current operational model. A current state value stream mapping exercise is essential to identifying the key frictions across the end-to-end flow of work. It may also reveal the critical activities that may be vulnerable to disruptions. For instance, if firms want to achieve end-to-end (E2E) supply chain visibility, it needs to understand the whole order-to-fulfilment process. Starting from the point when customers place an order, 'walk' through all the necessary activities until the order is fulfilled and delivered at customer's site. The supply chain diagnostic methodology known as *quick scan* discussed by Naim et al. (2002) can be used as a systematic approach to identify the change management opportunities in supply chains.

If we use the analogy of water flowing through a pipeline as information flows in the supply chain, we would expect the smoother the water (i.e. information/data) flows through the pipeline, the easier it is for the E2E visibility to be acquired. If there are many blockages in the 'water' pipeline, it typically means there is a heavily siloed information flow in place. Figure 7.5 provides a current state map of a telecoms manufacturing supply chain with orders (components) being shipped from the manufacturing sites (or imports) to a regional warehouse, then via a local 3PL depot, arriving at the client's partner site before they are delivered to the designated site for use. As can be observed, while the material flows are fairly straightforward, the information flow is much more complicated, causing significant delays and inefficiencies. As information flow dictates the movement of materials, streamlining the information flow can ultimately lead to improvements in the physical order fulfilment practice. Naturally, a digital transformation initiative should then target the problems with the information flow and explore potential digital solutions that could improve the current situation.

However, it can be dangerous to jump straight into digital solutions. In some cases, the processes themselves need to be scrutinised first before overlaying digital systems onto them. Questions need to be asked, for instance, using lean concepts: whether there are non-value-adding activities in current practice, and, if so, whether processes need to be streamlined before we restructure the associated information flows. Several generic methodologies exist to ensure a repeatable process to simplify existing complex operations, which was summarised by Watson (1994) as UDSO:

1. Understand: define the problem, system boundaries and performance metrics.
2. Document: model existing operations, whether in written, verbal, diagrammatical, mathematical, software or combined format.
3. Simplify: utilise the current state model to eliminate waste in all its forms (i.e. time, material, information and capacity).

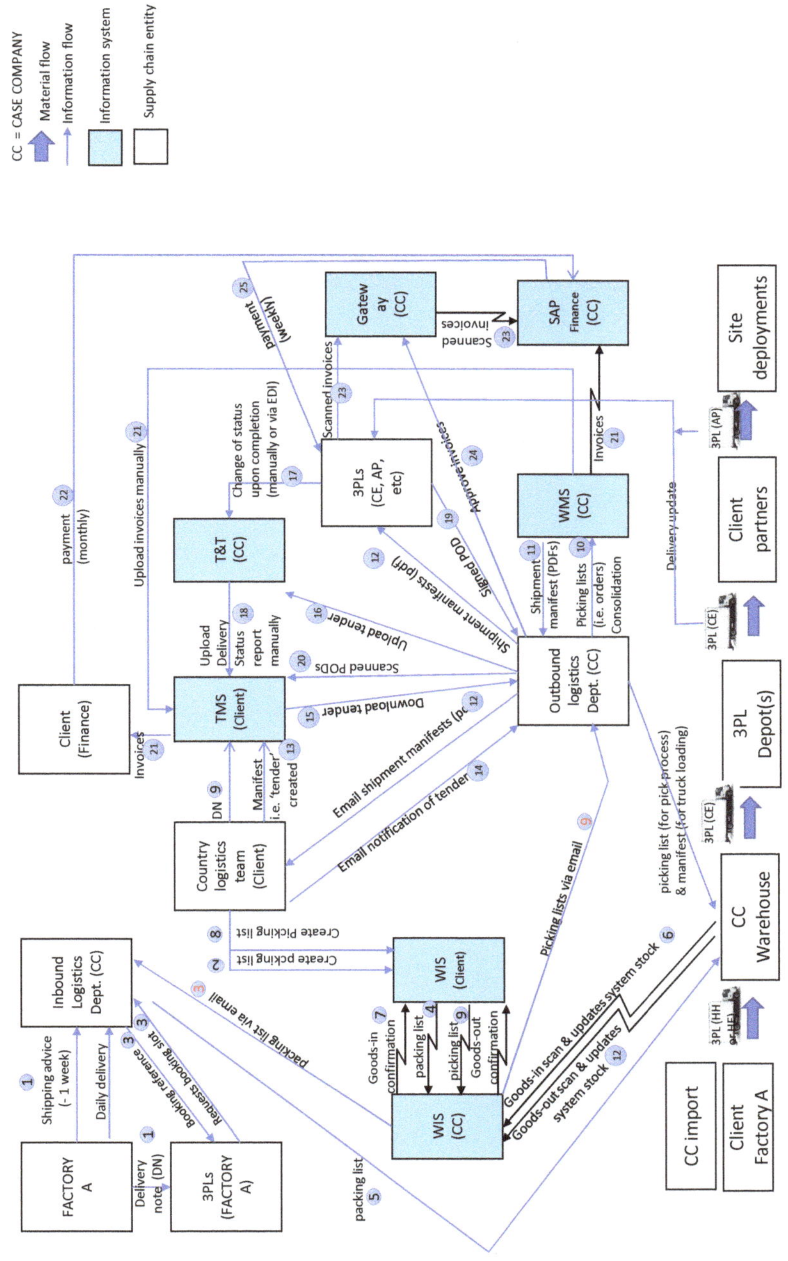

Figure 7.5: An example of current value stream map (information and material flows). Source: Authors.

4. Optimise: only once the processes have been identified and streamlined should advanced methods of control using digital tools can be applied to ensure consistency, reliability and transparency.

The simplicity paradigm is powerful, as quoted in Naim et al. (2002): 'Good managers can manage complexity, but better managers simplify.' It should be noted that implementing digital solutions usually demands changes in existing processes; for instance, implementing an ERP system in a multinational company will force the processes in local regions to be standardised. Therefore, process reengineering and digital solutions should go hand in hand.

In many cases, when it comes to supply chain digital transformation, firms need to ensure that their supply chain ecosystem partners are on board. Sometimes improvement may need to look beyond current process and capability improvement and involves supply chain structural adjustment (e.g. from offshore to near-shore). Consequently, when it comes to information integration, where is the appropriate place to begin? A common approach suggested by the academic literature is that a company should focus on internal integration first, move on to integration with suppliers, and then with customers (Horn, Scheffler & Schiele 2014; Stevens & Johnson 2016). However, supply chain models no longer focus on linear integration between customers and suppliers; we need to increasingly consider the ecosystem concept and us digital platforms (often powered by cloud computing) to achieve agile and flexible connectivity and collaboration.

Finally, under the process pillar, it is also important to consider the issues of having the right KPIs in place so that it can be determined whether a digital initiative delivers what is expected. Performance measures drive people's behaviours and therefore need to be designed carefully to be in line with the companies' strategy and goals.

Change Management

Change management is a well-established discipline in its own right. There are many change management models in academic and practice literature. Galli (2018) provided a detailed discussion about some of those models. One notable framework is the eight-step change model proposed by Kotter (1996; 2012) (Figure 7.6), which articulates how to manage change.

The original eight-step model is described as follows:

1. Establish a sense of urgency: people will not change if they cannot see the need to do so. Without motivation, people will not help, and the effort goes nowhere.
2. Create a guiding coalition: this step requires an organisation to assemble a group with power energy as change agent to chief the change effort and encourage the group to work together as a team.

1. Create a sense of urgency.	2. Create a core coalition.	3. Develop and form a strategic vision.	4.Communicate and share vision plans.
5.Empowering employees to act on the vision.	6.Generate short-term wins.	7.Consolidate gains and produce more change.	8. Initiate and set new changes.

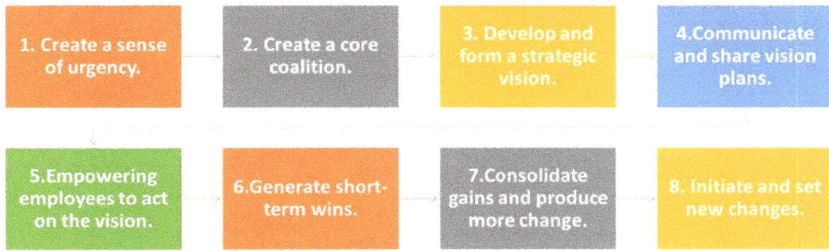

Figure 7.6: Eight-step change model. Source: Kotter (1996).

3. Develop a vision and strategy: create a vision of what the future will look like and how it will be achieved.
4. Communicate the change vision: tell people, in every possible way and at every opportunity, about the why, what and how of the changes.
5. Empower others to act on the vision: the first action in this step requires the removal of any obstacles to the change, and also allocating money, time and support needed to make change effective.
6. Generate short-term wins: complete transformation may take a long time so a loss of momentum is a major barrier to effective change management. Creating a lighthouse case, make the improvement from change visible, recognising and rewarding those involved is critical.
7. Consolidate gains and produce more change: this is a snowball approach. Kotter warns 'do not declare victory too soon'. Create momentum for change by building on successes in the change, invigorate people through the changes and develop people as change agents.
8. Anchor new approaches in the corporate culture: this is critical to long-term success and institutionalising the changes, so the new approaches become 'the way we do things around here'. Otherwise changes achieved through hard work and effort may slip away, with people reverting to the old and comfortable ways of doing things.

Another notable model is the data-driven business transformation road map by Gartner (Duncan 2020), which argues that becoming a data-driven enterprise requires explicit and persistent organisational change management to achieve measurable business outcomes. Senior executives need to promote cultural change and orchestrate 'leadership moments' in which they act as role models, exemplifying new cultural traits at critical points. Central to their success will be the ability to guide the workforce by addressing both data literacy ('skills') and data-driven culture ('will').

Bearing some similarity to Kotter's model, Duncan (2020) suggested a five-step road map. The starting point will be to sell the value and drive organisational awareness and ideation. Although supply chain leaders recognise the inherent need for data-driven decision-making, linking this need to specific benefits and outcomes can be challenging. The measurable value of digital transformation needs to be clearly articulated to both internal and external stakeholders. Step 2 moves to envisioning – develop vision and value propositions and communicating what stakeholders will get in return. Step 3 is about current state assessment in collaboration with HR and line of business leaders, particularly about data literacy and cultural readiness. Step 4 focuses on education, to devise curriculum and training plans. The last step focuses on embedding – launch and execute the transformational change programme. In a similar way to Kotter, Duncan argued that quick wins and basic changes to address immediate pain points build momentum and help recruit a 'coalition of the willing'. But he also cautioned that lasting, meaningful change takes time, because it requires the changing of mindsets and behaviours, the learning and practising of new skills, coordination and discipline, as well as the incentivising of people to participate.

Conclusion

In conclusion, we reflect here on the impact of emerging technologies on supply chains. It is clear from the range of examples presented throughout this monograph that the impact in the coming decades is going to be both far-reaching and extensive. Only organisations that are able to adapt their business models and adopt information technology systems in an effective way will survive. Leveraging and exploiting systems more widely will lead to greater competitive advantage, the reshaping of supply chain management, improvement in service speeds and reliability, the lowering of operating costs and improvements in efficiency. Positive adaptation to change will be fundamental to the success of many businesses and it will be important for supply chain organisations to understand the strategic value of ICT and assess what the impact on performance could be.

To address the issue of how data and digital capabilities can be used to create new value for existing and new customers, the concept of customer-centricity and the quest for sustainable supply chain outcomes and competitiveness have been shown to be the primary drivers of supply chain digital transformation. Aligning customer journeys with technology solutions, bringing the wider supply chain stakeholders on board and asking where your supply chain will be in the future will allow supply chain executives to innovate and focus. While digital technology is part of the solution to achieving supply chain goals, it is not an end in itself. Any organisation that is serious about a 'digital transformation project' will need to set this in the context of a robust business model. The three key pillars of data and technology, people and process discussed earlier in this chapter could be utilised to make sure a systematic approach is in place and help to identify gaps in current capabilities. All supply chain digital transformation will experience barriers and challenges and have setbacks. That is why we suggest that change management be at the heart of a transformation journey. Capturing and sharing the learnings as well as best practices throughout the journey is key to scale up and sustain the positive changes from the transformation.

The rate of advance in ICT will also create a range of challenges in the future. Data protection and governance will be important issues. With data becoming a strategic asset, organisations that control the flow of data will be increasingly under scrutiny. While governments will seek to limit the extent of such control through legislation, organisations are often more agile in how they respond, seeking to stay several steps ahead of any potential curtailing of their business models. Issues relating to the restriction of liberty and freedom at both personal and corporate levels will almost certainly become more prominent. Countries with centralised command-and-control economies already use ICT in ways that countries with democratic accountability are not. The interface between opposing approaches is likely to lead to a reshaping of how business is conducted. Companies involved in global supply chains will have to engage with and confront such issues. There is a continuing need to stress-test systems to understand where issues are likely to occur and how problems can be avoided, and, if not avoided, how negative outcomes can at least be suppressed. Risk management and supply chain resilience is of critical importance, and should be strategically embedded in any digital transformation programme, in response to a range of ever-increasing disruptions from pandemics (e.g. the Covid-19 crisis), cybercrime (e.g. the 2017 NotPetya attack), incidents (e.g. the 2021 Suez Canal blockage by the cargo ship *Ever Given*), natural disasters (e.g. the 2011 Japan tsunami) and geopolitical uncertainties (e.g. Brexit, 2020).

References

Bonnet, D. & Westerman, G. (2021). The new elements of digital transformation. *MIT Sloan Management Review, 62*(2), 82–89.

Boutetière, H., Montagner, A. & Reich, A. (2018). Unlocking success in digital transformations. Retrieved from: https://www.mckinsey.com/business-functions/organization/our-insights/unlocking-success-in-digital-trans formations [accessed June 2021].

Buvat, J., Solis, B., Crummenerl, C., Aboud, C., Kar, K., El Aoufi, H. & Sengupta, A. (2017). *The digital culture challenge: Closing the employee-leadership gap. Capgemini Digital Transformation Institute Survey*. Paris: Capgemini Digital Transformation Institute.

Catlin, T., Lorenz, J-T., Sternfels, B. & Willmott, P. (2017). A roadmap for a digital transformation. Retrieved from: https://www.mckinsey.com/industries/financial-services/our-insights/a-roadmap-for-a-digital-transformation [accessed December 2020].

Duncan, A. D. (2020). Roadmap for data literacy and data-driven business transformation: A Gartner trend insight report. Retrieved from: https://

www.gartner.com/document/3991368?ref=solrAll&refval=295022867 [accessed December 2020].

Eldor, L. (2021). Leading by doing: Does leading by example impact productivity and service quality? *Academy of Management Journal, 64*(2), 458–481.

Galli, B. J. (2018). Change management models: A comparative analysis and concerns. *IEEE Engineering Management Review, 46*(3), 124–132.

Günther, W. A., Mehrizi, M. H. R., Huysman, M. & Feldberg, F. (2017). Debating big data: A literature review on realizing value from big data. *The Journal of Strategic Information Systems, 26*(3), 191–209.

Hartley, J. L. & Sawaya, W. J. (2019). Tortoise, not the hare: Digital transformation of supply chain business processes. *Business Horizons, 62*(6), 707–715.

Horn, P., Scheffler, P. & Schiele, H. (2014). Internal integration as a pre-condition for external integration in global sourcing: A social capital perspective. *International Journal of Production Economics, 153*, 54–65.

House, R. J. (1977). A theory of charismatic leadership. In J. G. Hunt & L. L. Larson (eds.), *Leadership: The cutting edge,* (pp. 189–207). Southern Illinois University Press, Carbondale, IL.

Johansen, B. (2020). *Full-spectrum thinking: How to escape boxes in a post-categorical future.* Berrett-Koehler Publishers, Oakland, CA.

Katzenbach, J. R., Steffen, I. & Kronley, C. (2012). Cultural change that sticks. *Harvard Business Review, 90*(7), 110–117.

Kotter, J. P. (1996). *Leading change.* Harvard Business School Press, Boston, MA.

Kotter, J. P. (2012). Accelerate! *Harvard Business Review, 90*(11), 44–52.

Leonardi, P. (2020). You're going digital – now what. *MIT Sloan Management Review, 61*(2), 28–35.

Li, F. (2020). Leading digital transformation: Three emerging approaches for managing the transition. *International Journal of Operations & Production Management, 40*(6), 809–817. DOI: https://doi.org/10.1108/IJOPM-04-2020-0202.

Martínez-Caro, E., Cegarra-Navarro, J. G. & Alfonso-Ruiz, F. J. (2020). Digital technologies and firm performance: The role of digital organisational culture. *Technological Forecasting and Social Change, 154*, 119962.

Mesaglio, M., Olding, E. & Ommeren, E. V. (2019). Toolkit: 2019 collection of 85 culture hacks from the real world. Gartner. Retrieved from: https://www.gartner.com/document/3971030?ref=gfeed.

Naim, M. M., Childerhouse, P., Disney, S. M. & Towill, D. R. (2002). A supply chain diagnostic methodology: determining the vector of change. *Computers & Industrial Engineering, 43*(1–2), 135–157.

NCSC. (2018). Supply chain security guidance. Retrieved from: https://www.ncsc.gov.uk/collection/supply-chain-security [accessed December 2020].

Parenty, T. J. & Domet, J. J. (2019). Sizing up your cyber risks. *Harvard Business Review, 97*(6), 102.

Russom, P. (2021). Best practices for designing your data lake. Gartner. Retrieved from: https://www.gartner.com/document/4001766?ref=solrAll&refval=294701003 [accessed May 2021].

SE. (2020). Company annual report 2020. Retrieved from: https://www.se.com/ww/en/about-us/investor-relations/regulatory-information/annual-reports.jsp [accessed June 2021].

Stevens, G. C. & Johnson, M. (2016). Integrating the Supply Chain … 25 years on. *International Journal of Physical Distribution & Logistics Management, 46*(1), 19–42.

Struckman, C., Reina, D., Gabrys, E. & Ramirez, J. (2020). Using Gartner's Culture PRISM to change culture. Gartner. Retrieved from: https://www.gartner.com/document/3982141?ref=gfeed [accessed July 2021].

Tekic, Z. & Koroteev, D. (2019). From disruptively digital to proudly analog: A holistic typology of digital transformation strategies. *Business Horizons, 62*(6), 683–693.

Thaler, R. & Sunstein, C. (2008). *Nudge: Improving decisions about health, wealth, and happiness.* Yale University Press, New Haven, CT.

Vial, G. (2019). Understanding digital transformation: A review and a research agenda. *The Journal of Strategic Information Systems, 28*(2), 118–144.

Wang, Y., Skeete, J. P. & Owusu, G. (2021). Understanding the implications of artificial intelligence on field service operations: A case study of BT. *Production Planning & Control*, 1–17.

Watson, G. H. (1994). *Business systems engineering: Managing breakthrough changes for productivity and profit.* John Wiley & Sons, New York, USA.

World Economic Forum. (2017). Technology and innovation for the future of production: Accelerating value creation. Retrieved from: https://www.weforum.org/whitepapers/technology-and-innovation-for-the-future-of-production-accelerating-value-creation [accessed December 2020].

World Economic Forum. (2018). Digital transformation initiative executive summary report. Retrieved from: https://reports.weforum.org/digital-transformation [accessed July 2021].

World Economic Forum. (2019). Data science in the new economy: A new race for talent in the fourth industrial revolution. Retrieved from: https://www.weforum.org/reports/data-science-in-the-new-economy-a-new-race-for-talent-in-the-fourth-industrial-revolution [accessed December 2020].

World Economic Forum. (2021). Digital culture: The driving force of digital transformation. Retrieved from: https://www.weforum.org/reports/digital-culture-the-driving-force-of-digital-transformation [accessed July 2021].

Index

Symbols

5G   7, 8, 129

A

AEO   32
agility   2, 4, 16, 19, 21, 23, 49, 52,
       86, 97, 127
AI   5, 7, 9, 10, 11, 16, 20, 39, 40, 43,
       45, 46, 47, 49, 50, 52, 58, 63,
       125, 126, 129, 130
ambient intelligence   8
Analytics-driven insight   64
anything-as-a-service   5
API   33
application programming
       interface   33
AR   11, 12
artificial intelligence   5, 9, 19, 21, 49,
       63, 64, 139
artificial neural networks   6
augmentation   1, 126

augmented reality   11, 18
authorised economic operators   32
automation   1, 6, 10, 11, 14, 20,
       28, 40, 59, 63, 93, 116,
       126, 130
autonomous vehicles   5, 6, 9, 116
AV   9

B

B2B   5, 27, 71
B2C   4
B2G   27
business to business   5, 27, 71
big data   3, 5, 7, 18, 62, 105,
       116, 129
blockchain   3, 4, 7, 12, 13, 14, 16,
       21, 23, 28, 29, 30, 31, 32, 33,
       34, 35, 36, 37, 63, 70, 75, 104
blockchain technology   4, 12, 13,
       14, 16, 21, 23, 29, 30, 32, 35,
       36, 37
business to consumer   4

C

car2go   9
constrained optimisation problem   52
change management   65, 127, 134, 138
chatbots   5
circular economy   3, 4, 21, 96
climate change   3
CLM   64
cloud computing   3, 5, 7, 8, 19, 63, 103, 129, 134
cognitive computing   64
Covid-19   2, 137
CPO   65, 66, 67, 68, 77
cross-border logistics   25
CSR   68, 78, 79
customer-centric supply chains   6
cyber security   7
cybercrime   6

D

data lake   126, 129, 138
data mining   43, 70, 129
days in inventory outstanding   62
deep learning   6
demand sensing   3, 4, 128
digital engagement   63
digital revolution   62
digital road map   126
digital twin   3, 6, 9
digital workforce enablement   64
digitalisation   16, 62, 67, 77, 86, 122
DIO   62
distributed ledger technology   7, 36
distributed manufacturing   95
DLT   12, 36
drones   5, 11, 43

E

E2E   132
EC   10, 17, 103
EDI   100
e-commerce   2, 5, 10, 91, 119

electronic data interchange   96
EGLS   105
end-to-end visibility   6, 23, 34, 104
E-Space   17, 81, 82, 86, 87, 88, 89, 90, 91, 93, 94, 95, 96, 97
European green logistics strategies   105

F

FF   24, 112
flexibility   2, 4, 7, 8, 16, 19, 21, 23, 50, 58, 86, 90, 91, 97
freight forwarders   24
future supply chain   1, 30, 125

G

GA   44
graphics processing unit   5
greenhouse gas   100
gross national product   99
GHG   100, 110
GL   43, 44
global supply chain management   16, 23
GNP   99
GPS   3, 7

H

hash function   29

I

IaaS   7
ICT   7, 18, 136, 137
immersive technologies   11
information technology   2, 19, 123, 136
infrastructure as a service   7
intelligent supply chains   5
internet of things   5, 129
inventory and parts optimisation   5
IoT   4, 7, 9, 20, 41, 48, 51, 59, 63, 104, 105, 116, 129
IT   2, 6, 16, 21, 23, 30, 31, 35, 63, 125

K

KG 109, 114
knowledge graphs 105
KPI 94

L

LCM 105
LoB 41
local sourcing 96
logistics network optimisation 5
LSP 82, 85, 86, 90, 91, 92, 94

M

M&A 65, 66, 67
machine learning 3, 5, 6, 9, 43, 59, 129
mergers and acquisitions 65
mixed reality 11
modern digital architecture 64
MR 11, 12
MRA 32
mutual recognition agreements 32

N

National Crime Agency 6, 20
National Cyber Security Centre 6, 20, 129
NCA 6
NCSC 6, 20, 129, 138
new business models 1, 7

O

on-demand warehousing 81

P

physical internet 104, 119
PaaS 7
permissioned ledger 13
pervasive computing 8, 21
PI 104, 116
platform as a service 7
port community systems 112
public ledger 13

R

resilient supply chains 2
RFI 83
RFID 3, 9
RFQ 83, 85
robotic process automation 63
robotics 6, 9, 10, 63
robots 5, 9, 10, 11, 12, 93
ROI 65
RPA 63
radio frequency identification 3

S

S&OP 62
SaaS 7
SCN 103, 104, 105, 116
SELIS 17, 102, 103, 104, 105, 115, 116
sentient computing 8
service level agreements 16, 40, 63
Shared European Logistics Intelligent Information Space 17, 116
single window system 23
SLA 40, 41, 46, 49, 51, 52, 55, 57, 105
smart contracts 12, 14, 31, 33, 105, 116
SME 7
social sustainability 4, 19, 20
software as a service 7
sales and operations planning 62
small and medium-sized enterprises 7
strategic deployment 41
supply chain connectivity 6
supply chain digital transformation 14, 123, 124, 125, 126, 128, 134, 136
Sustainable Development Goals 3, 21, 73
sustainable supply chains 3

T

T&L   103, 104, 116
technology service providers   7
TradeLens   32, 33, 34, 37
transport and logistics   17, 103, 118
truck platooning   5
TSP   7

U

ubiquitous computing   8
UNECE   26, 27, 37, 119
United Nations Economic
    Commission for Europe   26
uTradeHub   27

V

virtual reality   11, 19
VR   11, 12

W

warehouse automation   6
WEF   127, 128, 130, 131
WMS   92
World Economic Forum   27, 36,
    127, 139

X

XaaS   5

www.ingramcontent.com/pod-product-compliance
Lightning Source LLC
Chambersburg PA
CBHW042120190326
41519CB00031B/7565